PEELED-BACK
Patchwork

Curves Without Piecing

Annette Ornelas

American Quilter's Society
P. O. Box 3290 • Paducah, KY 42002-3290
www.americanquilter.com

Located in Paducah, Kentucky, the American Quilter's Society (AQS) is dedicated to promoting the accomplishments of today's quilters. Through its publications and events, AQS strives to honor today's quiltmakers and their work and to inspire future creativity and innovation in quiltmaking.

EDITOR: TERI COFFMAN
GRAPHIC DESIGN: ELAINE WILSON
COVER DESIGN: MICHAEL BUCKINGHAM
PHOTOGRAPHY: CHARLES R. LYNCH

Library of Congress Cataloging-in-Publication Data
Ornelas, Annette.
    Peeled-back patchwork : curves without piecing / by Annette Ornelas.
        p. cm.
    Includes bibliographical references.
    ISBN 1-57432-858-1
  1. Patchwork--Patterns. 2. Quilting--Patterns. 3. Circle in art. I. Title.

    TT835.O75 2004
    746.46'041--dc22

                    2004016671

Additional copies of this book may be ordered from the American Quilter's Society, PO Box 3290, Paducah, KY 42002-3290; 800-626-5420 (orders only please); or online at www.americanquilter.com. For all other inquiries, call 270-898-7903.

Dedication

This book is dedicated to my husband, Mike, who makes all things possible and encourages me to follow my heart. Thank you for your love and for supporting my creative spirit.

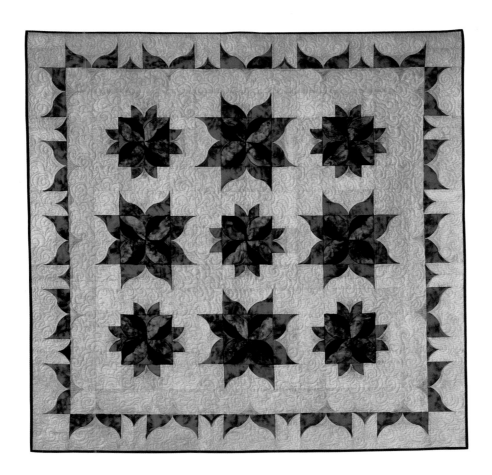

Acknowledgments

Thank you to my family, Mike, Nicole, Derrick, and Kyle, for supporting my endeavors, and a special thank you to my mother, Annedore, for stitching endless bindings.

I am grateful to all my workshop students who continue to inspire me and are always willing to try yet another one of my ideas. Thank you for providing me with so much over the years – clever questions, encouragement, and your valuable input. Without students there are no teachers, and teaching and finding solutions to questions is what I like most of all.

A special thank you goes to Iris Noitalay, from Iris's Quilt Garden, for quilting the larger quilts for this book. I also want to give thanks to Marian Cornell, Paquita McCreery, Iris Noitalay, Karen Potts, and Helona Wheeler for trying out and making quilts for this book, and to Beth Berghoff and Karen Potts for reading chapters and patterns and contributing their editing skills.

Thanks to all the members of my Art Quilt Group for all their input and suggestions, and to my local quilt shop, Loving Stitches, and their staff, for all their encouragement and help. They never get tired of helping me find that special fabric I usually need right away.

Thank you, Bali Fabrics, Inc., Princess Mirah Design, for batik fabrics.

Many thanks to Barbara Smith, Teri Coffman, and Elaine Wilson.

Contents

Introduction

Curves have always fascinated me. They seem to make a quilt come alive like no other element, while forming the perfect complement to squares and triangles. For me, the linear geometry of angular quilt blocks combined with the gentleness of a curved design reveals a special harmony. However, conventional curved piecing methods seem to be unpopular among quilters. Trying to fit the convex and concave pieces together just the right way requires experience, making curved piecing a technique reserved for the intermediate and advanced quilter.

Since beginning to quilt, I have always looked for better techniques to make any quilt block easier to piece. I like to design and execute all my quilts quickly, without much difficulty. This often requires a certain amount of creativity to get around more complex seams like insets and curves. My search for an easier curved seam led me to dimensional curved piecing. This technique makes it possible for quilters of all skill levels to do straight-line patchwork piecing with curved results. This is accomplished by incorporating folded shapes into the seams and turning the folds back on themselves to reveal curved designs.

In the patterns presented, I will lead you from simple through intermediate to advanced designs. If you follow this path, you will certainly be able to accomplish all the designs, and you can incorporate folded curves in many other traditional blocks to dramatically change the appearance of your quilts.

chapter

1

General Instructions

Fabric Selection

The most important thing about fabric selection is to choose good quality 100 percent cotton fabrics. Fabric blends like polyester-cotton shrink at a different rate than cotton. Therefore, they may make your piecing inaccurate. This problem gets compounded every time the fabric is ironed. Think of all the time you invest in your quilts and think about how long you would like for your quilts to last.

I prefer bright, high-contrast fabrics. Batiks are great fabrics to use for many of the designs. Most batik fabrics have no right or wrong side and are lightweight, which is a great advantage when folding and layering. I also like to use tone-on-tone fabrics, which lend an extra glow to quilts and make them look less flat and more interesting.

Should you wash your fabrics? There are pros and cons for washing your fabrics before using them in a quilt. Washing removes the sizing. This may be essential to quilters with chemical sensitivities. On the other hand, washing will make the fabrics softer and difficult to crease and work with when making dimensional curved designs.

To test your fabrics for colorfastness, snip off a corner and dip it in hot water. While it is dripping wet, place this fabric corner on a white paper towel and check for bleeding after it has dried. If there is any bleeding, wash the fabric and retest it before you use it in your quilt, particularly if that quilt is used on a bed or as a cover that will be washed frequently.

For a wallhanging that you know will not be washed, prewashing may not be necessary. If you make a wallhanging from unwashed fabric and decide to give it as a gift, you can include a "dry clean only" label to let the recipient know that it is not a good idea to wash this quilt.

Some of the quilts presented feature a scrappy look. This is your chance to delve into your fabric stash and use up some of your scraps. You can use a multitude of fabrics as long as you follow a few simple guidelines. Many fabrics of similar values are interchangeable. Overall, fabrics substituted for one color should have similar values. That doesn't mean you can't throw in an occasional accent to wake up the eyes. Another way to make an easy scrappy quilt is to substitute one fabric with a multitude of monochromatic fabrics. For example, instead of one blue, use many different blues.

Many new quilters approach fabric selection from the standpoint of decorating or clothing. This usually results in quilts that are too matched. A lot of quilts are representations of geometric pictures and it is important to work with contrast rather than blending all the colors. Contrast shows off the quilt design and adds some drama to your quilt.

For beginning quilters, it may be helpful to look at multi-print fabrics that have designs. Select a fabric that gets your attention, one that talks to you. Pick one that catches your eye, whether or not it matches your couch. Are the colors used in the fabric design pleasing? If you like the colors, use them as a guide for choosing other fabrics for your quilt. This will help you achieve a harmonious look.

Color value, in light, medium, or dark, is one of the most important considerations when picking fabrics. So in addition to picking the right colors, pay attention to the value of the fabric. A sufficient value contrast between fabrics is needed to effectively show the designs.

Dimensional Curved Piecing

Dimensional piecing is a technique of layering and inserting folded fabric pieces into the seam lines of a pieced unit or block. When the bias edge of a folded square (folded in half diagonally) is turned back and stitched down, a curve appears. The curved edge is then secured by topstitching close to the fold. This technique lets you do complicated-looking designs with ease.

All the patterns presented include dimensional inserted shapes. Examples of curved shapes include the dimensional centers in DESERT BLOOM (page 47), BEADED PRIMROSE (page 72), FAIRY FLOWERS (page 80), and the dimensional squares in SPINNING WHEELS (page 34).

Tools

For dimensional piecing, your glue-stick will quickly become your new best friend. It takes the place of pinning and is used to temporarily secure the folded shapes on top of other fabric pieces. Using a glue-stick is an easy and fast way to keep the pieces from slipping, and it

helps to ensure accuracy. Any glue-stick is acceptable as long as it washes out of the fabric. Look for one that says "washable" on the label.

Masking tape may be used to temporarily secure two folded pieces. When making dimensional centers, the two folded pieces must meet in the center. The best way to secure them and keep them from shifting is to use a strip of masking tape. You could, of course, use pins or a glue-stick, but pins can distort the shape, and the glue-stick can be applied only when there is no danger of it showing on the front of the quilt after unfolding the shapes. Sometimes little things can make a big difference.

Universal needles work well for most sewing, but they are not sharp enough for the specialized piecing techniques and multiple fabric layers we are sewing. For dimensional curved piecing, I prefer to use quilting needles for both piecing (size 75/11) and quilting (size 90/14).

For best results, the threads used for topstitching the curves should be of good quality and should match the curved fabrics. Use matching embroidery-weight cotton thread to make your topstitching less visible. Sulky® 40-weight rayon, Madeira® rayon Classic No. 60, or the newest polyester threads also work well, especially when you cannot find a suitable color in a cotton thread. However, these do tend to call more attention to the stitching line on the curves. For virtually invisible stitches, use monofilament thread, which is also good for scrap quilts in which the colors or values change from block to block.

Pressing Folded Shapes

Folding squares. Place a fabric square on your ironing board, wrong side up. Fold one corner to the opposite corner (fig. 1–1). Touch the piece briefly with your iron to set the fold.

To streamline the folding, you can place as many squares, side by side, as will fit comfortably on your ironing board. Fold and press a square in half diagonally and leave the iron on it briefly while folding the next square, and so on. This is a huge timesaver and makes all this pressing more fun and efficient.

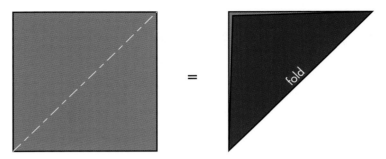

Fig. 1–1. Fold the square in half diagonally.

Folding rectangles. Place a fabric rectangle on the ironing board, wrong side up. Fold the rectangle in half so the short sides are together (fig. 1–2). Press lightly with an iron. You can streamline press these pieces also.

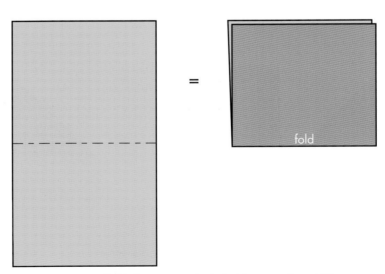

Fig. 1–2. Fold the rectangle in half across its width.

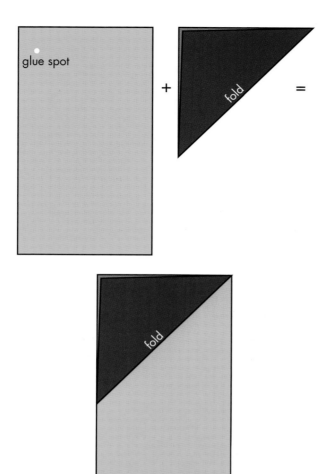

Fig. 1–3. Place the glue where it won't show.

Layering and Sewing

Here comes the fun part, layering and sewing folded shapes into seams.

Triangle units. Place a folded square on a larger square or rectangle of a different color and align the raw edges as shown in figure 1–3. Secure the folded piece with a dab of glue. Be sure to place the glue opposite the side with the folded edge so that the glue spot will not show when the piece is turned, curved, and stitched. This layered piece will be treated as a single unit.

Flying Geese. For dimensional Flying Geese, use a glue-stick to secure two folded squares to a rectangle (fig. 1–4). Notice that one folded square overlaps the other.

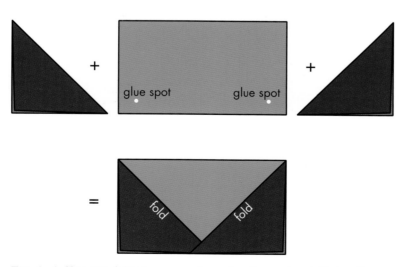

Fig. 1–4. Use two folded squares to make dimensional Flying Geese.

Y-shaped units. Creating Y-shaped units is like making a sandwich. You place a folded rectangle in between two larger squares or rectangles. There are three different units that can be made with this method. In figure 1–5a, you can see how the raw edges of the folded rectangle are aligned at the top edge to make each type of unit. Add the top piece (face down) to each unit. Then stitch through all three layers with a ¼" seam allowance, catching the folded piece in the seam (fig. 1–5b). Open the unit and press it flat (fig. 1–5c). Open the seam allowances in the back to reduce bulk.

Y-shaped unit with squares

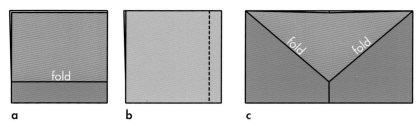

Y-shaped unit with vertical rectangles

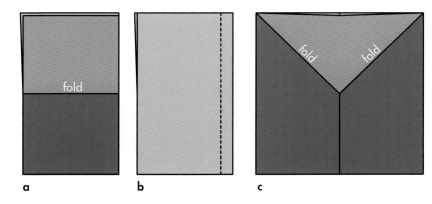

Y-shaped unit with horizontal rectangles

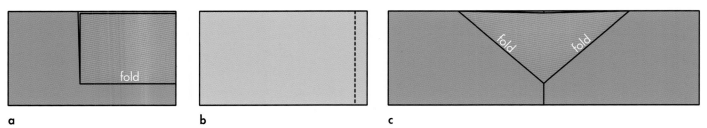

Fig. 1–5. Three types of Y-shaped units: **(a)** Place a folded rectangle on the bottom piece aligning the raw edges as shown, **(b)** Add the top piece and sew the layers together. **(c)** Open the resulting piece and press.

Tips

• To avoid problems when putting your blocks together and setting them into your quilt, remember that you need a ¼" seam allowance around each unit.

• Sewing over many layers of fabric can present a challenge for some sewing machines. What to do if you get stuck? No problem: lift your presser foot, advance or scoot your fabric piece back ¹⁄₁₆" to ⅛", drop the presser foot, and continue sewing.

Pressing to Reduce Bulk

During the construction of your quilt, use a dry iron. Steam tends to distort your piecing. Use your iron gently and press rather than iron your fabric pieces. You can use steam when the quilt is completed if some of the pieced areas do not lie entirely flat.

For folded inserts, press the seam allowances in the direction they want to go. If multiple fabric layers come together in one seam, press the seam allowances open to distribute the bulk evenly on both sides and to make them lie flat.

Nesting Seam Allowances

When you are piecing blocks together, often the seam allowances no longer lie in opposite directions for matching seams. This is easily remedied by flipping one of the seam allowances in the other direction while sewing. Don't worry, the quilt police won't get you for this.

I often need to flip my seam allowances to have them nest or lock together. Using this flipping technique will make your piecing a lot easier to sew and smoother. On the back of your quilt, you can see a twist in the seam allowance (fig. 1–6). Usually that is no great worry unless you want to quilt in the ditch. If this flipped seam bothers you (I usually just flatten it with my iron), make a tiny snip with your scissors close to the crossing seam and fold the offending seam allowance back the other way. Be careful not to snip all the way to the stitching line.

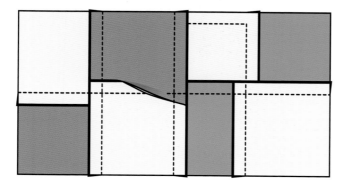

Fig. 1–6. Twisting seam allowances is sometimes necessary to make them nest for matching seams.

Curving the Inserts

Single curves. To help you curve a folded dimensional insert as you topstitch it, you can use your sewing machine needle as a third "hand." Insert the needle where you want to start sewing the curve. If you have a needle-down function on your sewing machine, this is the time to use it. Carefully pull back the bias edge of the folded shape and smooth it into a curve. Begin sewing by stitching in place to secure the stitches. Stitch along the curved fold with a normal straight stitch (fig. 1–7). Sew close to the folded edge but be careful not to "fall off" the curved edge. End the topstitching by stitching in place to secure your threads.

If you can use the same thread color for the next fabric shape to be turned, don't snip the threads between shapes. Raise your presser foot, travel to the next fold, and pull your threads to the next piece. Curve and topstitch it. Clip the threads after each color to avoid getting tangled when stitching with the next thread color.

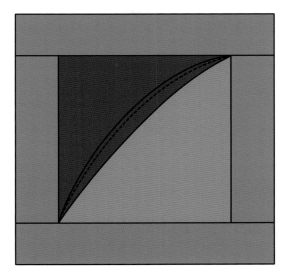

Fig. 1–7. To curve a folded insert, fold the bias edge back and topstitch.

DIMENSIONAL PINWHEEL block, page 25

Double curves. SPINNING STARS (page 55) and ENCHANTED ROSE GARDEN (page 63) feature folded triangles with double curves. To make these, secure the center of the bias fold with a pin. Pull back the first half of the bias edge. Start the stitches, securing them by stitching in place. Stitch along the fold with a straight stitch up to the pin (fig. 1–8). Remove the pin, pull back the remaining bias edge and continue stitching to the corner. Secure your threads by stitching in place.

Overlapping Curves. To topstitch, insert the needle in one end of the first bias edge at the triangle point (fig. 1–9a). Stitch in place to secure your threads. With the needle down, fold back the first bias edge to make a curve (fig. 1–9b). Topstitch along the curve (fig. 1–9c). Stop about ⅛" to ¼" before you reach the end of the first fold. Pull back and lap the second fold over the first fold and make one stitch to hold the second fold in place (fig. 1–9d). You may have to hand-walk the sewing machine to make this first stitch accurately. Continue stitching to the other side of the unit. Stitch in place to secure your threads. You now have a completed curved Y-shaped unit (fig. 1–9e).

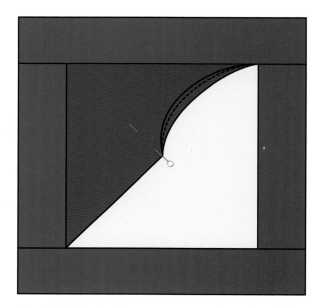

Fig. 1–8. For double curves, use a pin to mark the center.

SPINNING STARS block, page 55

Overlapping Curves

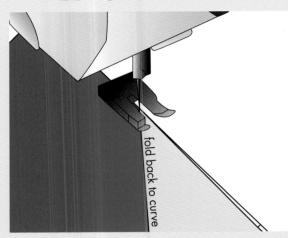

Fig. 1–9. (a) Begin stitching at one end of the triangle.

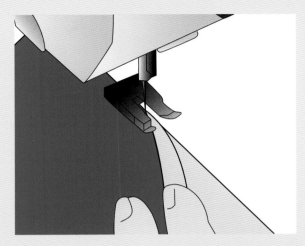

Fig. 1–9. (b) With the needle down, fold back the bias edge in a curve.

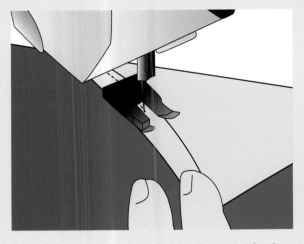

Fig. 1–9. (c) Topstitch along the curved edge. Stitch close to the fold. Stop approximately ⅛" from the pivot point.

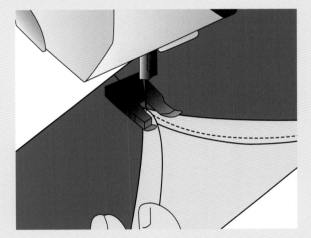

Fig. 1–9. (d) Fold the second bias edge over the first one and continue stitching.

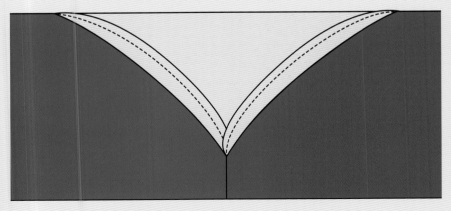

Fig. 1–9. (e) Completed Y-shaped unit

Fig. 1–10. Star-point unit

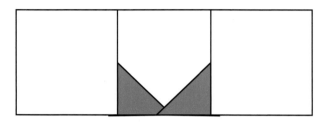

Fig. 1–11. Sew the units and squares in rows.

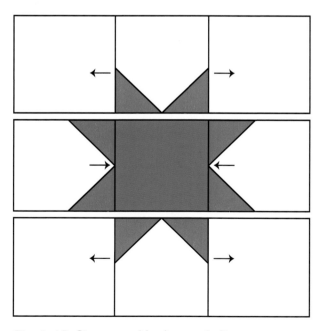

Fig. 1–12. Star assembly. Arrows indicate seam allowance pressing.

Super-Simple Folded Stars

Have you ever struggled with making star points come out just right? Here is a super simple solution that is easy and a lot faster than the traditional approach. Cut the following pieces to make one 6" star in a 9" background piece. To simplify things, our star block will have three colors: red, white, and blue.

Red star points – 8 squares 2"
Blue star center – 1 square 3½"
White background – 8 squares 3½"

1. Take all your red fabric squares to your ironing board. Lay the squares side by side, wrong side up. Fold the squares in half diagonally and press the fold with a warm iron.

2. Place two folded triangles on the bottom corners of a white 3½" square, with raw edges aligned, as shown in figure 1–10. Secure the triangles with a dab of glue. Notice how the triangles overlap at the bottom for the seam allowance. Make four star-point units.

3. Sew the star-point units and blue and white squares together in horizontal rows (fig. 1–11). Press the seam allowances of the top and bottom rows toward the white corner squares. Press the seam allowances of the middle row toward the blue center square.

4. Join the rows to finish the star (fig. 1–12). Press the last two seam allowances between the rows open to reduce bulk.

Voilà. You did it!

chapter

The Patterns

PATRIOTIC STARS

PATRIOTIC STARS, 47½" x 59½", made by the author

PATRIOTIC STARS

Skill level: BEGINNER

Finished block size: 9"

Finished quilt size: 47½" x 59½"

The techniques in PATRIOTIC STARS include super-simple folded stars, triangle units, and Y-shaped units. The quilt is easy and fast to make and a perfect gift for anyone.

Before beginning, review Fabric Selection (page 8) and Dimensional Curved Piecing (page 10). Y-shaped unit construction is described on page 13.

Yardage and Cutting Requirements

Yardage (42" wide fabric)	First Cut (cut strips across the width)	Second Cut
Dark red ¾ yd.	3 strips 2" 6 strips 2" (inner border) 1 strip 3½"	48 squares 2" (piece C) ---- 6 squares 3½" (piece E)
Medium light red ⅜ yd.	4 strips 2"	48 rectangles 2" x 3½" (piece B)
Medium light blue 1½ yds.	5 strips 2" 1 strip 3½" 6 strips 6" (outer border)	96 squares 2" (piece F) 12 squares 3½" (piece H) ----
Light background 1⅜ yds.	2 strips 2" 11 strips 3½"	24 rectangles 2" x 3½" (piece A) 42 squares 3½" (piece D) 27 rectangles 3½" x 9½" (piece G)
Binding ½ yd.	6 strips 2"	
Backing 3 yds.	2 pieces 32" x 52"	
Batting (90" wide) 1½ yds.	1 piece 51" x 63"	

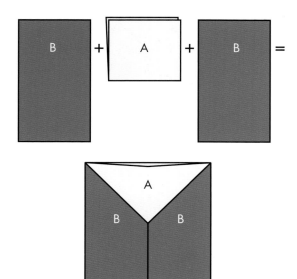

Fig. 2–1. Y-shaped unit

Making Red Star Blocks

1. Fold the A rectangles in half. Fold the C squares diagonally. (Dimensional pieces are always folded right side out.)

2. Sew a folded A rectangle between two B rectangles to make a Y-shaped unit (fig. 2–1). Make 24.

3. Use a glue-stick to secure two folded C squares to each Y-shaped unit, as shown in figure 2–2.

4. Sew the E and D patches together with the units to complete a Star block. Press the last two seam allowances open to reduce bulk. Make six.

5. Curve the A pieces (fig. 2–4, page 23). Do not curve the C pieces.

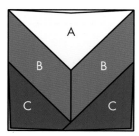

Fig. 2–2. Add two folded C squares.

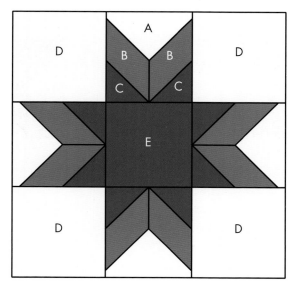

Fig. 2–3. Star block

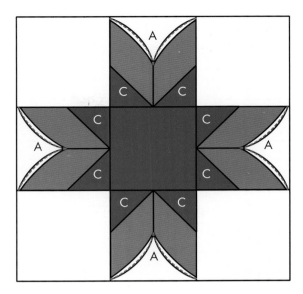

Fig. 2–4. Curve the A inserts.

Making Blue Star Units

1. Fold the F squares in half diagonally. Use a glue-stick to secure two folded F squares on a D square (fig. 2–5). Make 14 units.

2. Glue four folded F squares on a G rectangle (fig. 2–6). Make 17 units.

Quilt Assembly

✦ Follow the quilt assembly diagram to lay out the blocks, units, and remaining patches (fig. 2–7, page 24). Sew the pieces into horizontal rows. Then sew the rows together.

✦ Cut two of the border strips in half. Sew a half strip to each of the long strips. Measure down the center of the quilt and cut two dark red inner border strips this length. Stitch these to the sides of the quilt. Measure across the center of the quilt. Cut the two pieced strips this length. Stitch them to the top and bottom.

✦ For the outer border, measure, cut, and sew the medium blue border strips as you did for the dark red border strip.

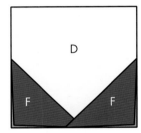

Fig. 2–5. D/F unit

Finishing

✦ Sew the backing pieces together along one long side.

✦ Layer the backing, batting, and quilt top. Quilt the layers. Leave the dimensional pieces unquilted so they will stand out.

✦ Join the binding strips end to end and bind the raw edges.

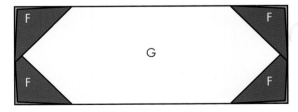

Fig. 2–6. F/G unit

Fig. 2–7. Quilt assembly

DIMENSIONAL PINWHEELS

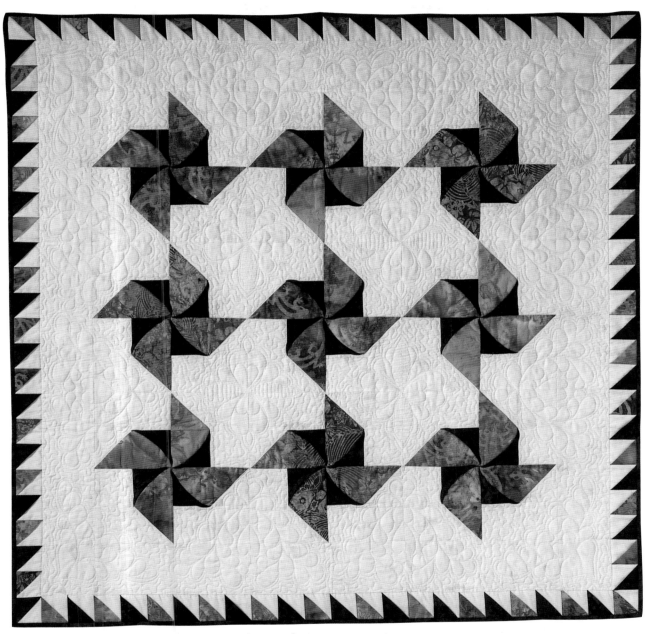

DIMENSIONAL PINWHEELS, 48½" x 48½", made by the author

DIMENSIONAL PINWHEELS

Skill level: BEGINNER
Finished block size: 12"
Finished quilt size: 48½" x 48½"

DIMENSIONAL PINWHEELS was developed with the beginning quilter in mind. It has a limited number of fairly large pieces, which can be put together very simply. Even the Sawtooth border is made with folded squares. Once you know how to make the Pinwheel block, you can easily expand this quilt by adding sashing or more borders.

Before beginning, review Fabric Selection (page 8) and Dimensional Curved Piecing (page 10).

Yardage and Cutting Requirements

Yardage (42" wide fabric)	First Cut (cut strips across the width)	Second Cut
Light 2⅛ yds.	3 strips 3½" 3 strips 6½" 6 strips 2½" 5 strips 4½"	36 squares 3½" (piece A) 36 rectangles 3½" x 6½" (piece D) 92 squares 2½" (piece H) 4 strips 4½" x 36½" (inner border) 4 squares 4½" (piece E)
Medium 1 yd.	3 strips 6½" 3 strips 2½"	36 rectangles 3½" x 6½" (piece B) 46 squares 2½" (piece F)
Dark ⅔ yd.	3 strips 3½" 3 strips 2½"	36 squares 3½" (piece C) 46 squares 2½" (piece G)
Backing 3 yds.	2 pieces 27" x 52"	
Binding ⅜ yd.	5 strips 2"	
Batting (90" wide) 1½ yds.	1 piece 52" x 52"	

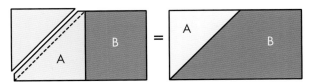

Fig. 2–8. A/B unit

Making Pinwheel Blocks

1. Mark a diagonal line on the wrong side of each A square. Place an A square on the left side of a B rectangle, right sides together. Sew on the marked diagonal line. Cut off the excess fabric ¼" beyond the stitching line. Flip the A piece back and press (fig. 2–8). Make 36.

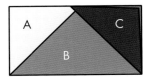

Fig. 2–9. A/B/C unit

2. Fold the C squares in half diagonally, right side out. Use a glue-stick to secure a folded C square on an A/B unit to make an A/B/C unit (fig. 2–9). Make 36.

3. Sew four A/B/C units and four D patches together to make a Pinwheel block (fig. 2–10). Make nine.

4. Curve the folded C squares (fig. 2–11).

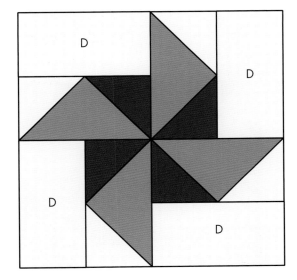

Fig. 2–10. Pinwheel block

Quilt Assembly

✦ Follow the quilt assembly diagram to sew three Pinwheel blocks together to make a row. Make three rows, then join the rows (fig. 2–12, page 28).

✦ For the inner border, sew two strips to the sides of the quilt. Stitch an E piece to both ends of the remaining strips and sew them to the top and bottom.

✦ For the outer border, fold the F and G squares into triangle shapes. Secure them on the H squares with a glue-stick. Make 92 border units.

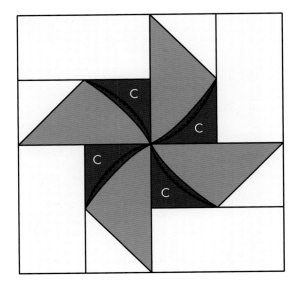

Fig. 2–11. Block with curves.

✦ For each side border strip, sew together 22 border units, alternating dark and medium folded squares. Sew these strips to the sides of the quilt and press the seam allowances toward the white border strips.

✦ For the top and bottom borders, join 24 units, rotating one end unit of each strip as shown in the quilt assembly diagram. Sew these strips to the top and bottom of the quilt.

Finishing

✦ Sew the backing pieces together along one long side.

✦ Layer the backing, batting, and quilt top. Quilt the layers. Leave the dimensional pieces unquilted so they will stand out.

✦ Join the binding strips end to end and bind the raw edges.

Fig. 2–12. Quilt assembly

HEART STRINGS

HEART STRINGS, 38½" x 44½", made by the author

Heart Strings

Skill level: BEGINNER
Finished block size: 6"
Finished quilt size: 38½" x 44½"

This simple little quilt will delight children of all ages. It is easy to make and can be made scrappy or more organized and elegant.

Before beginning, review Fabric Selection (page 8) and Dimensional Curved Piecing (page 10). Y-shaped unit construction is described on page 13.

Yardage and Cutting Requirements

Yardage (42" wide fabric)	First Cut (cut strips across the width)	Second Cut
Light background 1¼ yds.	11 strips 2"	60 squares 2" (piece C) 30 rectangles 2" x 6½" (piece D) 30 rectangles 2" x 3½" (piece A)
	5 strips 3½"	60 squares 3½" (piece E)
Assorted medium and dark* 1 yd.	8 strips 3½"	60 rectangles 2" x 3½" (piece B) 30 rectangles 3½" x 6½" (piece F)
Border ⅝ yd.	4 strips 4½"	
Backing 1½ yds.	1 piece 42" x 48"	
Binding ⅜ yd.	5 strips 2"	
Batting (90" wide) 1¼ yds.	1 piece 42" x 48"	

*You may want to match the B and F rectangles for each heart.

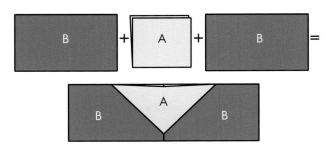

Fig. 2–13. A/B Y-shaped unit

Making Heart Blocks

1. Fold the A and F rectangles in half. Fold the C squares in half diagonally. (Dimensional pieces are always folded right side out.)

2. Sew a folded A rectangle between two B rectangles to make a Y-shaped unit, as shown in figure 2–13. Make 30.

Fig. 2–14. Add two folded C squares.

3. To complete the top of the heart, glue one folded C square on both ends of each unit (fig. 2–14).

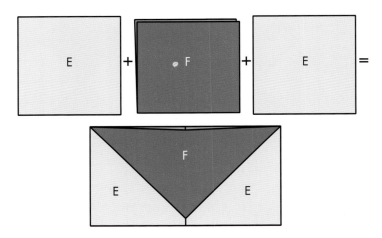

4. For the bottom of the heart, sew a folded F rectangle between two E squares to make a Y-shaped unit (fig. 2–15). Make 30.

5. Join the Y-shaped units and a D patch to make a Heart block as shown in figure 2–16. Make 30. (You can streamline your heart production by chain piecing, if you like.)

Fig. 2–15. E/F Y-shaped unit

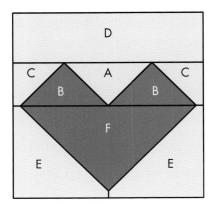

Fig. 2–16. Heart block

Fig. 2–17. Quilt assembly

Assembling the Quilt

◆ Follow the quilt assembly diagram (fig. 2–17) to join the blocks. To add the border, measure down the center of the quilt and cut two border strips this length. Sew these to the sides of the quilt. Measure across the center of the quilt, and cut two border strips this length. Sew them to the top and bottom.

◆ Curve the inserts (fig. 2–18). If you are using only one thread color or invisible monofilament, sew the tops of the hearts in each horizontal row in one long continuous curve. Sew the bottom of the hearts in each row the same way.

Finishing

◆ Layer the backing, batting, and quilt top. Quilt the layers. Leave the dimensional pieces unquilted so they will stand out.

◆ Join the binding strips and bind the raw edges.

Design Wall Play

◆ If you are using many different fabrics for the hearts, a design wall allows you to play with the placement of your blocks. You may even want to make a few extra blocks to audition. Blocks not used may be sewn into small quilts, doll quilts, or other projects.

◆ When you are not sure about a color, leave your quilt blocks on the design wall and walk by them a few times. A fabric that does not fit will be quickly identified and may be changed before it makes its way into your quilt.

Fig. 2–18. Curve the tops of the hearts across each row, then the bottoms on the return pass.

SPINNING WHEELS

SPINNING WHEELS, 57" x 75", made by the author

SPINNING WHEELS

Skill level: INTERMEDIATE
Finished block size: 9"
Finished quilt size: 57" x 75"

SPINNING WHEELS is a great scrap quilt featuring a Churn Dash block that is dramatically changed to a wheel shape after the folded squares are curved. This is the perfect quilt to make if you want to dig into your fabric stash and use up some of your scraps. You can make it as scrappy as you like as long as you use block colors that contrast with the background. For scrap quilts, always cut a few extra block pieces. Then, you can pick and choose, and you won't be limited when selecting your fabrics.

You can easily change the size of this quilt it by making more or fewer blocks for the center and borders. To keep the design symmetrical, use an odd number of blocks in each horizontal and vertical row in the center of the quilt. For example, set the blocks three by three, five by five, five by seven, etc.

Before beginning, review Fabric Selection (page 8) and Dimensional Curved Piecing (page 10).

Yardage and Cutting Requirements

Yardage (42" wide fabric)	First Cut (cut strips across the width)	Second Cut
Light value background 4¼ yds.	20 strips 3½"	196 squares 3½" (piece A) 10 rectangles 3½" x 9½" (piece F)
	7 strips 6½"	8 squares 6½" (piece G) 20 rectangles 6½" x 9½" (piece H)
	3 strips 9½"	10 squares 9½" (piece I)
Medium value scraps 1 yd. (SPINNING WHEELS has blue, green, magenta, and gold scraps)	7 strips 3½"	76 squares 3½" (piece B)
	2 strips 2"	1 strip 2" x 16" (four-patches) 14 squares 2" (piece D)
Dark value scraps ¾ yd. (SPINNING WHEELS has dark purple scraps)	5 strips 3½"	56 squares 3½" (piece C)
	2 strips 2"	1 strip 2" x 16" (four-patches) 14 squares 2" (piece E)
Backing 3⅝ yds.	2 pieces 40" x 61"	
Binding ½ yd.	7 strips 2"	
Batting (90" wide) 1¾ yds.	1 piece 61" x 79"	

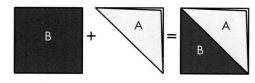

Fig. 2–19. A/B unit

Fig. 2–20. A/C unit

Making Churn Dash Blocks

1. Fold 32 A squares in half diagonally. Use a glue-stick to secure each folded A triangle on a B square to make A/B units (fig. 2–19). (Dimensional pieces are always folded right side out.)

2. Fold 32 C squares in half to make a rectangle shape. Glue each folded C square on an A square to make A/C units (fig. 2–20).

3. Follow Figure 2–21 to make eight Churn Dash blocks.

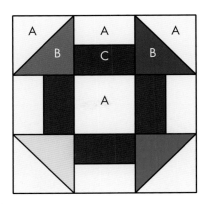

Fig. 2–21. Churn Dash block

Making Alternate Blocks

1. To make the four-patches for the centers of the alternate blocks, join the medium and dark 2" x 16" strips along one long side to make a strip-set. Press the seam allowances toward the dark strip.

2. Cut 14 segments, each 2" wide, from the strip-set (fig. 2–22a). Join the segments to make seven four-patches (fig. 2–22b).

3. Fold 14 D and 14 E squares in half diagonally. Glue a folded D or E shape to opposite corners of each A square (fig. 2–23). Make 14 A/D units and 14 A/E units.

4. Join units and A patches to make an alternate block (fig. 2–24). Make 7 .

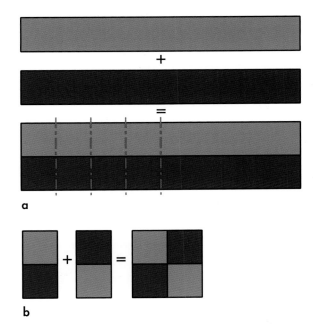

Fig. 2–22. Making four-patches. **(a)** Cut the strip-set into 2" segments. **(b)** A completed four-patch unit.

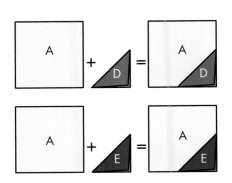

Fig. 2–23. (a) A/D unit (b) A/E unit

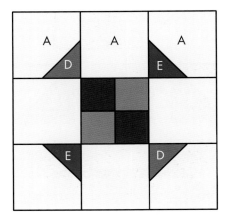

Fig. 2–24. Alternate block

Fig. 2–25. Curved A squares

Curving the Blocks

1. Curve the folded A squares in each Churn Dash block (fig. 2–25).

2. You may also curve the inserts in each alternate block. Whether stitched down or left loose, these triangles add to the overall dimensional appearance of the quilt.

Making Border Units

1. Fold 44 A squares in half diagonally. Use a dab of glue to secure each folded A square on top of a B square to make 44 A/B units (fig. 2–26).

2. Fold the remaining C squares into rectangle shapes. Glue each folded C square on top of an A square to make 24 A/C units (fig. 2–27).

3. Refer to figure 2–28 to make the border pieces.

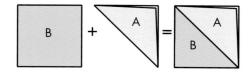

Fig. 2–26. A/B unit

Fig. 2–27. A/C unit

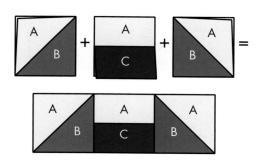

Fig. 2–28. (a) Border side unit. Make 16.

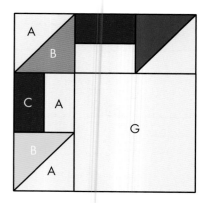

Fig. 2–28. (b) Border corner. Make 4.

Assembling the Quilt

✦ Follow the quilt assembly diagram to arrange the blocks and the G, H, and I pieces (fig. 2–29). Note that the rotation of the four-patches changes from row to row.

✦ Curve adjacent A inserts in a continuous stitching line. When the A pieces aren't adjacent, simply drag the threads to the next one.

Finishing

✦ Sew the backing pieces together along one long side.

✦ Layer the backing, batting, and quilt top. Quilt the layers. Leave the dimensional pieces unquilted so they will stand out.

✦ Join the binding strips end to end and bind the raw edges.

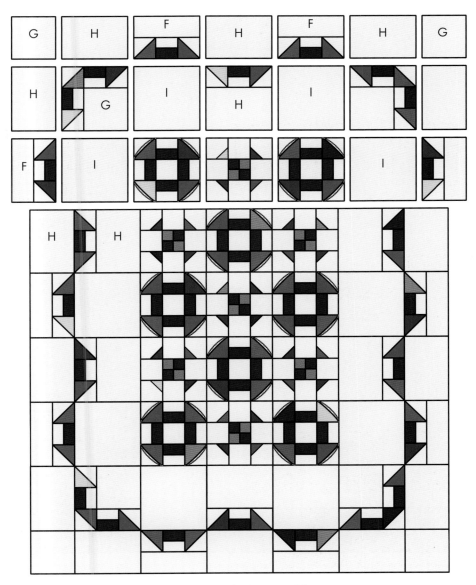

Fig. 2–29. Quilt assembly

SPARKLING STARS

SPARKLING STARS, 64" x 80", made by Iris Noitalay, Fayetteville, North Carolina

Peeled-Back Patchwork ~ Annette Ornelas

SPARKLING STARS

Skill level: INTERMEDIATE
Finished block size: 12"
Finished quilt size: 64" x 80"

SPARKLING STARS features my dimensional approach to stars. The folded star points are easy enough for any beginner to make. To put a new spin on an old favorite, I designed a curved Hourglass block to separate the Star blocks. The design in the center of the quilt spills over into the pieced border, which rounds off and frames the stars.

When choosing fabrics for this quilt, pay attention to the light, medium, and dark values. Look for a contrast between the green, red, and multi-print background, and create an even greater contrast between the stars and their backgrounds. You can easily enlarge the quilt by adding border strips.

Before beginning, review Fabric Selection (page 8) and Dimensional Curved Piecing (page 10). Y-shaped unit construction is described on page 13.

Yardage and Cutting Requirements

Yardage (42" wide fabric)	First Cut (cut strips across the width)	Second Cut
Light beige 1 yd.	8 strips 2½" 2 strips 4½"	128 squares 2½" (piece E) 16 squares 4½" (piece H)
Medium gold ¾ yd.	6 strips 2½" 2 strips 4½"	96 squares 2½" (piece A) 12 squares 4½" (piece D)
Medium red 3¾ yds.	9 strips 2½" 12 strips 8½"	48 rectangles 2½" x 4½" (piece B) 48 squares 2½" (piece C) 48 rectangles 4½" x 8½" (piece J)
Dark green 3 yds.	12 strips 2½" 8 strips 8½"	64 rectangles 2½" x 4½" (piece F) 64 squares 2½" (piece G) 64 rectangles 4½" x 8½" (piece I)
Medium-dark multi-print 2⅜ yds.	4 strips 4½" 4 strips 8½" 2 strips 12½"	28 squares 4½" (piece K) 14 squares 8½" (piece L) 4 squares 12½" (piece M)
Backing 4 yds.	2 pieces 42" x 68"	
Binding ⅝ yd.	8 strips 2"	
Batting (90" wide) 2 yds.	68" x 84"	

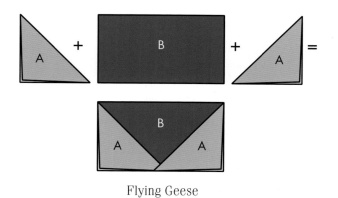

Flying Geese

Making Star Blocks

This quilt contains two differently colored blocks. One has gold stars on a red background, and the other has beige stars on a green background.

1. Fold the gold A and beige E squares in half diagonally. (Dimensional pieces are always folded right side out.)

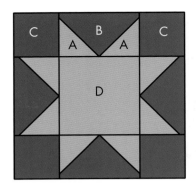
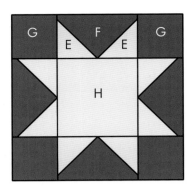

Fig. 2–30. (a) Gold and red block, (b) beige and green block.

2. To make dimensional Flying Geese, use a glue-stick to secure two folded A squares on each red B and two folded E squares on each green F (fig. 2–30 and Flying Geese, page 42).

3. Follow figure 2–30 to make 12 gold and red Star blocks and 16 beige and green Star blocks.

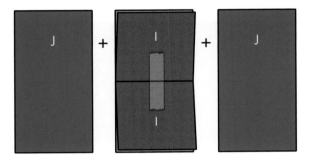

Fig. 2–31. Tape the folded I pieces together before inserting them between the J rectangles.

Making Hourglass Blocks

1. For each Hourglass block, fold the I rectangles in half, right side out. Press.

2. Position and tape two I pieces with the folds meeting in the middle (fig. 2–31).

3. Sandwich the two folded I pieces between two J rectangles, right sides together, and stitch along the right edge with a ¼" seam allowance (fig. 2–32).

Fig. 2–32. Sew the sandwich layers together.

4. Unfold the unit and pull the folded I pieces open to form triangles (fig. 2–33). Make 17 Hourglass blocks. Reserve leftover folded I pieces for the border blocks.

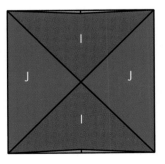

Fig. 2–33. Hourglass block

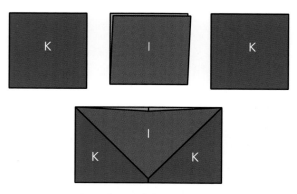

Fig. 2–34. Border star unit

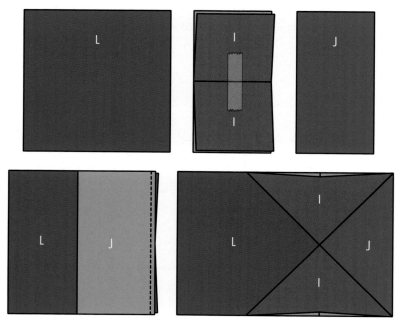

Fig. 2–35. Sew border unit to star.

Fig. 2–36. Border hourglass unit

Making Border Units
Border star unit

✦ For each border star unit, layer and sew one folded I piece between two K squares to make a Y-shaped unit (fig. 2–34). Make 10 units.

✦ Sew a border star unit to 10 of the beige Star blocks, as shown in figure 2–35.

Border hourglass unit

For each unit, position and tape two I pieces with the folds meeting in the middle. Place the I pieces on the L square. Place a J rectangle on top and sew the pieces together. Open the unit and press (fig. 2–36). Make six units.

Border right-side unit

Press eight K squares in half diagonally. For each unit, place a folded I and a folded K on an L square, as shown in figure 2–37. Place a J rectangle on top and sew the pieces together. Open the unit and press. Make four units.

Border left-side unit

For each unit, place a folded I and a folded K on an L square, as shown in figure 2–38. Place a J rectangle on top and sew the pieces together. Open the unit and press. Make four units.

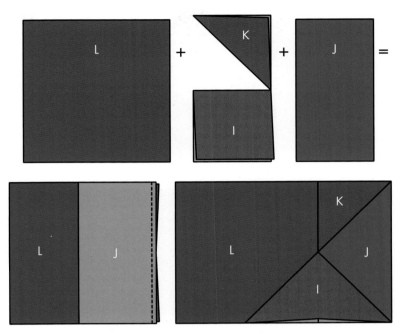

Fig. 2–37. Border right-side unit

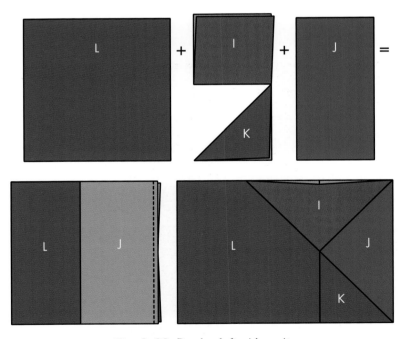

Fig. 2–38. Border left-side unit

left-side unit   right-side unit

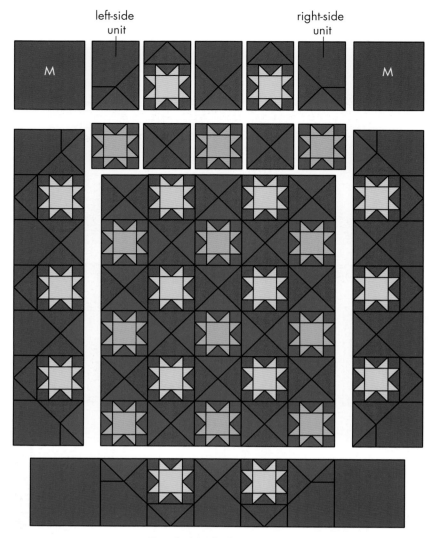

Fig. 2–39. Quilt assembly

Assembling and Finishing

✦ Follow the quilt assembly diagram (fig. 2–39) for this step. For the center of the quilt top, join the Star and Hourglass blocks into rows. Then join the rows.

✦ Join the border units, as shown, to make two side border strips. Sew these to the sides of the quilt.

✦ To make remaining border strips, join the units and M pieces. Sew these to the top and bottom of the quilt.

✦ Curve the inserts in the Hourglass blocks (fig. 2–44) and border units. (You can topstitch around each star design or sew continuously in diagonal rows.)

✦ Stitch the backing pieces together along the edges.

✦ Layer the backing, batting, and quilt top. Quilt the layers. To make the Hourglass curves stand out, leave the dimensional pieces unquilted.

✦ Join the binding strips and bind the raw edges.

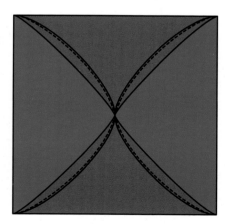

Fig. 2–40. Topstitch the bias folds to secure the curves.

DESERT BLOOM

DESERT BLOOM, 48½" x 60½", made by the author

DESERT BLOOM

Skill level: INTERMEDIATE
Finished block size: 6"
Finished quilt size: 48½" x 60½"

DESERT BLOOM is made in the soft colors of the Southwest. It looks complex because it has six blocks, but you will be surprised how simple it is to make.

Before beginning, review Fabric Selection (page 8) and Dimensional and Curved Piecing (page 10). Y-shaped unit construction is described on page 13.

Yardage and Cutting Requirements

Yardage (42" wide fabric)	First Cut (cut strips selvage to selvage)	Second Cut
Medium-light green ½ yd.	3 strips 2"	48 squares 2" (piece C)
	5 strips 1¼" (inner border)	----
Dark purple 1¼ yds.	8 strips 2"	52 squares 2" (piece A)
		58 rectangles 2" x 3½" (piece L)
	5 strips 4½" (outer border)	----
Medium-light pink ⅝ yd.	8 strips 2"	20 squares 2" (piece G)
		82 rectangles 2" x 3½" (piece H)
Medium-dark magenta ⅔ yd.	5 strips 2"	56 squares 2" (piece B)
		24 rectangles 2" x 3½" (piece K)
	5 strips 1¾" (middle border)	----
Orange ¼ yd.	3 strips 2"	28 squares 2" (piece D)
		10 rectangles 2" x 3½" (piece F)
Light 1⅜ yds.	8 strips 3½"	48 rectangles 3½" x 6½" (piece E)
	7 strips 2"	48 rectangles 2" x 3½" (piece I)
		48 squares 2" (piece J)
Backing 3 yds.	2 pieces 32" x 53"	
Binding ½ yd.	6 strips 2"	
Batting (90" wide) 1½ yds.	53" x 65"	

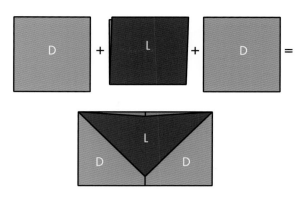

Fig. 2–41. Y-shaped unit

Making Blocks
Flower block 1

1. Fold the L rectangles in half, right side out. Layer and sew one folded L piece between two D squares, as shown in figure 2–41, to make a Y-shaped unit. Make 12.

2. Place two folded L pieces between two Y-shaped units, as shown in figure 2–42. (Pin or tape the folds so the pieces don't move during sewing.) Sew the pieces together, then press them open to make the flower center. Make six.

3. Add C and H patches to the flower centers, as shown in figure 2–43, to complete each flower block. (Pay careful attention to matching the triangle points at the corners.) Make six.

4. Curve the inserted L pieces (fig. 2–44).

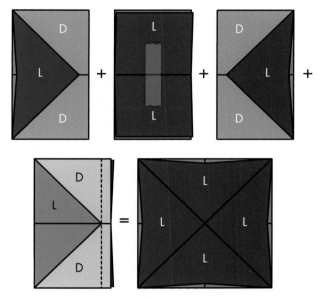

Fig. 2–42. Flower center

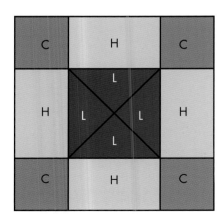

Fig. 2–43. Flower block 1

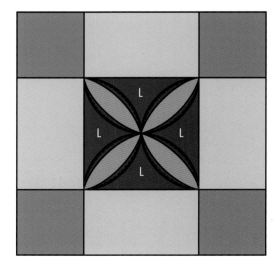

Fig. 2–44. Block with curved L pieces.

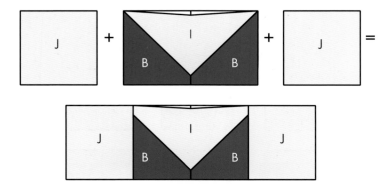

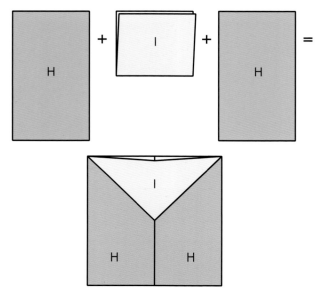

Fig. 2–45. B/I/J unit

Flower block 2

1. Fold the I and K rectangles in half.

2. Layer and sew one folded I piece between two B squares to make a Y-shaped unit. Add a J square to each end of the unit (fig. 2–45). Make 24.

3. Layer and sew one folded I piece between two H rectangles to make a Y-shaped unit (fig. 2–46). Make 24.

Fig. 2–46. H/I unit

4. Place two folded K pieces between two H/I Y-shaped units, as shown in figure 2–47. (Pin or tape the folded K pieces together so they don't move during sewing.) Sew along the right edge, then press the unit open. Make 12.

5. Join two B/I/J units and one H/I/K unit to complete Flower block 2 (fig. 2–48). Make 12.

6. Curve the inserted K pieces (fig. 2–49). Wait to curve the inserted I pieces until the blocks have been joined.

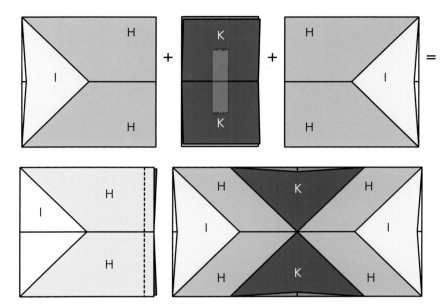

Fig. 2–47. H/I/K unit

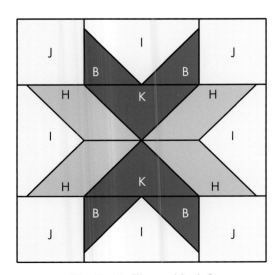

Fig. 2–48. Flower block 2

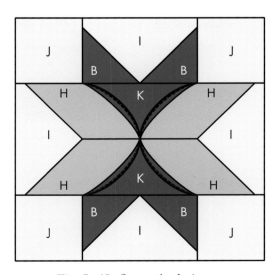

Fig. 2–49. Curve the I pieces.

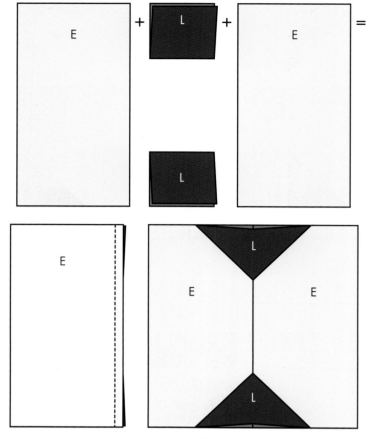

Fig. 2–50. Double Y-shaped unit

Alternate block

Place two folded L pieces between two E rectangles, as shown in figure 2–50. Sew along the right edge to make a double Y-shaped unit. Make 17.

Half block 1

1. Fold the F rectangles in half. Sew one folded F piece between two A squares to make a Y-shaped unit (fig. 2–51). Make 10.

2. Add C, G, and H patches, as shown in figure 2–52, to complete the half block. Make 10.

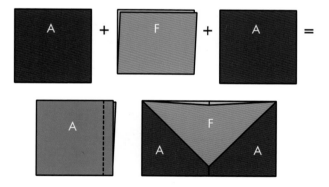

Fig. 2–51. Y-shaped unit

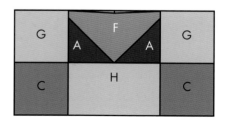

Fig. 2–52. Half block 1

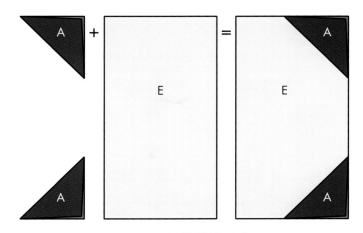

Half block 2

Fold 28 A squares in half diagonally. Use a glue-stick to secure two folded A triangles on each E rectangle as shown in figure 2–53. Make 14.

Fig. 2–53. Half-block 2

Corner block

Fold four D squares in half diagonally. Join A, B, and C squares to make a four-patch unit. Use a glue-stick to secure the folded D squares on the A square to complete the block (fig. 2–54). Make four.

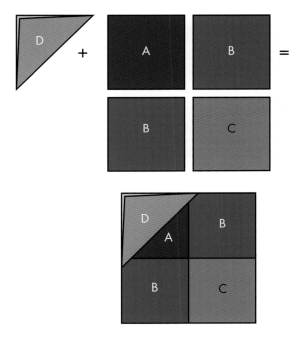

Quilt Assembly

✦ Refer to the quilt assembly diagram (fig. 2–55, page 54) to arrange the various blocks. Sew the blocks together in horizontal rows. Then join the rows.

✦ Complete the curving of all remaining dimensional pieces, except the ones along the raw edges of the quilt.

✦ For the inner border measure across the center of the quilt and cut two green border strips this length. Stitch these to the top and bottom of the quilt.

Fig. 2–54. Corner block

Fig. 2–55. Quilt assembly

✦ Cut one of the remaining green border strips in half . Sew a half strip to each of the long strips. Measure down the center of the quilt. Cut the two pieced strips this length and sew them to the sides of the quilt.

✦ For the middle border, measure, cut, and sew the magenta border strips as you did for the green border strips. Likewise, measure, cut, and sew the purple strips in the same way for the outer border.

Finishing

✦ Curve the remaining inserts along the outer edges of the quilt.

✦ Sew the backing pieces together along one long edge.

✦ Layer the backing, batting, and quilt top. Quilt the layers. Leave the dimensional pieces unquilted so they will stand out.

✦ Join the binding strips and bind the raw edges.

SPINNING STARS

SPINNING STARS, 44½" x 60½", made by the author

SPINNING STARS

Skill level: Intermediate
Finished Spinning Star block size: 12"
Finished Windmill block size: 4"
Finished quilt size: 44½" x 60½"

SPINNING STARS is the perfect size for a baby or crib quilt. Because of its primary colors, this quilt is equally suitable for both boys and girls. To make a more definite baby boy quilt, use blue in the binding. Use red for a baby girl or gold if you don't know if the baby-to-be is a boy or a girl.

Before beginning, review Fabric Selection (page 8) and Dimensional and Curved Piecing (page 10). Y-shaped unit construction is described on page 13.

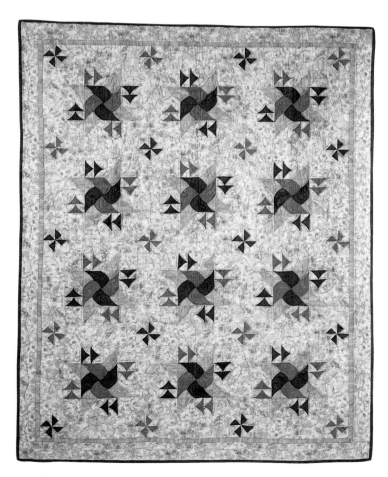

Alternate quilt setting, made by Marian Cornell, Southern Pines, North Carolina

Yardage and Cutting Requirements

Yardage (42" wide fabric)	First Cut (cut across the width)	Second Cut
Light background 1⅛ yd.	5 strips 2" 4 strips 3½" 4 strips 2½"	96 squares 2" (piece H) 48 squares 3½" (piece J) 96 rectangles 1½" x 2½" (piece L)
Medium-dark red ½ yd.	3 strips 3½" 1 strip 2½"	36 rectangles 2" x 3½" (piece B) 12 squares 3½" (piece F) 24 rectangles 1½" x 2½" (piece G)
Medium-dark blue ½ yd.	3 strips 3½" 1 strip 2½"	36 rectangles 2" x 3½" (piece D) 12 squares 3½" (piece E) 24 rectangles 1½" x 2½" (piece I)
Medium gold ⅝ yd.	4 strips 2" 2 strips 3½"	24 squares 2" (piece A) 24 rectangles 2" x 3½" (piece C) 24 squares 3½" (piece K)
Light blue 1⅝ yds.	6 strips 4½" 5 strips 4½" (border)	17 rectangles 4½" x 12½" (piece M)
Backing 2⅞ yds.	2 pieces 33" x 49"	
Binding ½ yd.	5 strips 2" x 42"	
Batting (90" wide) 1⅜ yds.	1 piece 49" x 65"	

Making Spinning Star Blocks

To prepare the folded pieces for all of the blocks, fold the A, E, F, and K squares in half diagonally, and fold the G and I rectangles in half. Also fold 24 B and 24 D rectangles in half. (Dimensional pieces are always folded right side out.)

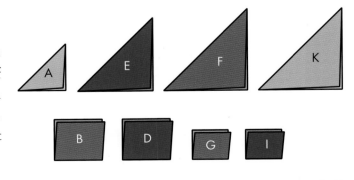

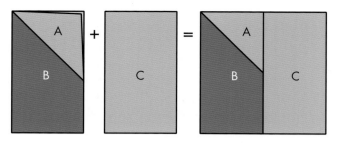

Fig. 2–56. A/B/C unit

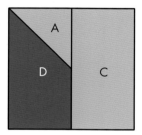

Fig. 2–57. A/C/D unit

Spinning star center

1. Use a glue-stick to secure a folded A square on a B rectangle. Sew a C rectangle to the right side of the A/B unit (fig. 2–56). Make 12.

2. Glue a folded A square on each D rectangle. Sew a C rectangle to the right side of each A/D unit (fig. 2–57). Make 12.

3. Refer to figure 2–58. Glue a folded E triangle on each A/B/C unit. Glue a folded F triangle on each A/C/D unit. Make 12 of each unit.

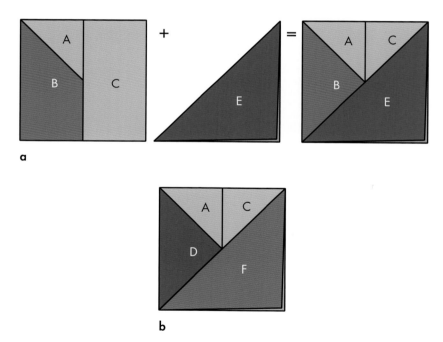

a

b

Fig. 2–58. Center units: **(a)** A/B/C/E center unit, **(b)** A/C/D/F center unit

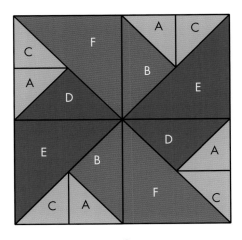

Fig. 2–59. Star center

4. Arrange the units in windmill fashion, alternating colors. Sew the units together to make a star center (fig. 2–59). Make six.

Spinning star frame

1. Sew a folded B piece between two H squares to make a red Y-shaped unit (fig. 2–60). Make 24.

2. Repeat step 1, substituting folded D pieces for the B pieces (fig. 2–61). Make 24 blue units.

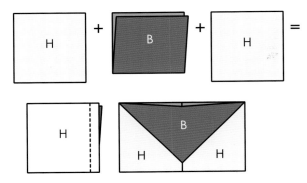

Fig. 2–60. Red Y-shaped unit

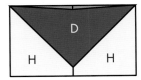

Fig. 2–61. Blue Y-shaped unit

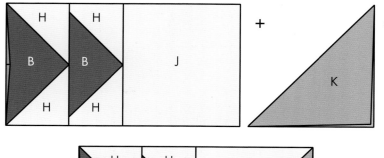

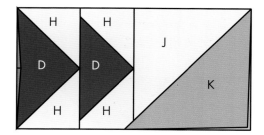

Fig. 2–62. Red frame unit

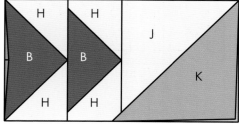

Fig. 2–63. Blue frame unit

3. Sew two red Y-shaped units together with a J square. Glue a gold folded K square to make a red frame unit (fig. 2–62). Make 12.

4. Repeat with two blue Y-shaped units and a folded K square to make a blue frame unit (fig. 2–63). Make 12.

Complete block

To complete the spinning star block, sew the star center, frame units, and J squares together, as shown in figure 2–64. Make six.

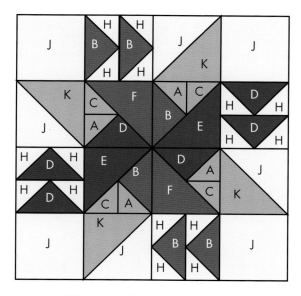

Fig. 2–64. Spinning star bock

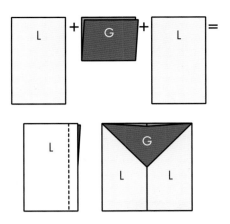

Windmill block

1. Sandwich a folded G rectangle between two L rectangles to make a red Y-shaped unit (fig. 2–65). Make 24.

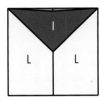

Fig. 2–65. Red Y-shaped unit

2. Repeat, substituting the blue I rectangles for the red G rectangles to make a blue Y-shaped unit (fig. 2–66). Make 24.

Fig. 2–66. Blue Y-shaped unit

3. For each block, arrange four units in windmill fashion, keeping the same colors together. Join the units to complete the windmill block (fig. 2–67). Make 6 of each color.

Quilt Assembly

✦ Follow the quilt assembly diagram (fig. 2–68, page 62) to join the spinning star blocks, windmill blocks, and M rectangles.

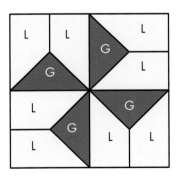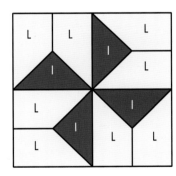

Fig. 2–67. Windmill block

✦ Curve the A, B, and D pieces in the Spinning Star blocks. Double curve the E, F, and K pieces also (fig. 2–69, page 62).

✦ Measure across the center of the quilt and cut two border strips this length. Sew these to the top and bottom of the quilt.

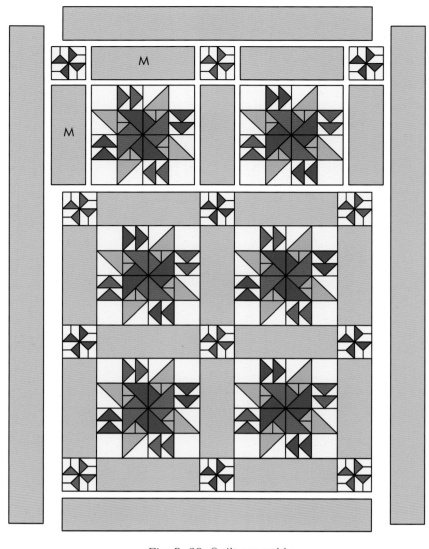

Fig. 2–68. Quilt assembly

✦ Cut one of the remaining border strips in half. Sew a half border to each long strip. Measure down the center of the quilt. Cut the two pieced strips this length and sew them to the sides of the quilt.

✦ Although it is not necessary, if you like, you can curve the inserts in the swirl blocks.

Finishing

✦ Stitch the backing pieces together along the edges.

✦ Layer the backing, batting, and quilt top. Quilt the layers. Leave the dimensional pieces unquilted so they will stand out.

✦ Join the binding strips and bind the raw edges.

✦ You can easily enlarge this quilt pattern by adding rows of blocks.

Fig. 2–69. Quilt with curved pieces

ENCHANTED ROSE GARDEN

ENCHANTED ROSE GARDEN, 51½" x 51½", made by the author
In this quilt, the Rosebud blocks and Large Flower blocks are set on point with sashing.

ENCHANTED ROSE GARDEN

Skill level: **ADVANCED**
Finished block size: 12"
Finished quilt size: 51½" x 51½"

ENCHANTED ROSE GARDEN is a two-block quilt with a rosebud and a large flower. The piecing for both blocks is similar, with the Rosebud block featuring a dimensional bud that makes the whole quilt come to life.

Before beginning, review Fabric Selection (page 8) and Dimensional and Curved Piecing (page 10). Y-shaped unit construction is described on page 13.

Yardage and Cutting Requirements

Yardage (42" wide fabric)	First Cut (cut across the width)	Second Cut
Light background 2½ yds.	17 strips 2"	40 squares 2" (piece D) 96 rectangles 2" x 3½" (piece G) 16 rectangles 2" x 6½" (piece I) 32 rectangles 2" x 5" (piece M)
	12 strips 3½"	40 squares 3½" (piece H) 16 rectangles 3½" x 9½" (piece J) 20 rectangles 3½" x 6½" (piece K)
	1 strip 5"	4 squares 5" (piece N)
Gold ¼ yd.	2 strips 3½"	40 rectangles 2" x 3½" (piece E)
Medium red 1 yd.	15 strips 2"	108 rectangles 2" x 3½" (piece C) 112 squares 2" (piece F)
Dark teal ½ yd.	3 strips 3½"	36 squares 3½" (piece A)
Medium green ⅝ yd.	4 strips 3½"	36 squares 3½" (piece B) 16 rectangles 2" x 3½" (piece L)
Binding ½ yd.	6 strips 2"	
Backing 3½ yds.	2 pieces 28" x 56"	
Batting (90" wide) 1⅝ yds.	56" x 56"	

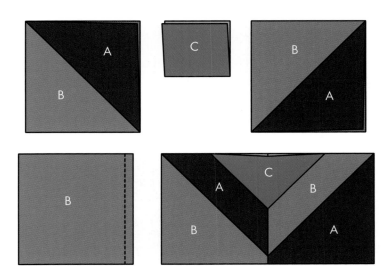

Fig. 2–70. A/B/C unit

Rosebud Blocks

Block center

1. Fold 20 A squares in half diagonally and fold 20 C rectangles in half. (Dimensional pieces are always folded right side out.)

2. Use a glue-stick to secure a folded A square on each B square. Make 20.

3. Refer to Y-shaped unit construction on page 13 and figure 2–70 to make the following unit. Sew a folded C rectangle between two A/B units to make an A/B/C unit. (Pay particular attention to the rotation of the A/B units.) Make 10.

4. Using Y-shaped unit construction, sew two folded C rectangles between two A/B/C units, as shown in figure 2–71, to complete a block center. Make five.

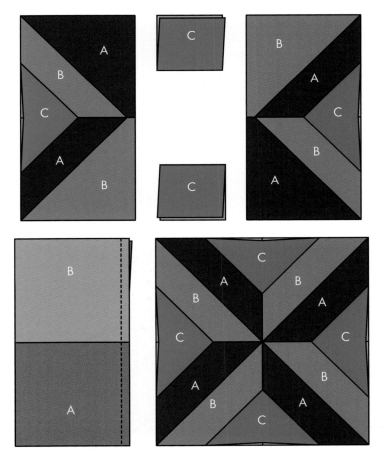

Fig. 2–71. Block center

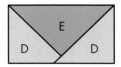

Fig. 2–72. Traditional Flying Geese unit (no folds)

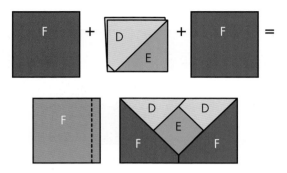

Fig. 2–73. D/E/F unit

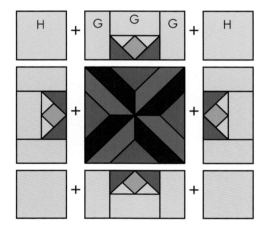

Fig. 2–74. Rosebud block

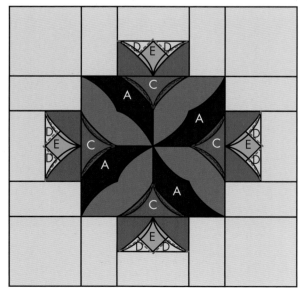

Fig. 2–75. Rosebud block with curves

Block frame

1. Mark a diagonal line on the wrong side of 40 D squares. Place a D square on the left side of an E rectangle, right sides together. Sew on the marked diagonal line. Cut off the excess fabric ¼" beyond the stitching line. Flip the D piece back and press. Repeat for other side of the E rectangle (fig. 2–72). Make 20.

2. Fold each traditional Flying Geese unit in half, right side out. Using Y-shaped construction, sew a folded Flying Geese unit between two F squares as shown in figure 2–73. Make 20 D/E/F units, four for each block.

Complete block

1. Sew the G rectangles to the D/E/F units. Then sew the units, block center, and H background squares together, as shown in figure 2–74, to complete a Rosebud block. Make five.

2. Curve the D/E and C pieces and double curve the A pieces (fig. 2–75). For another

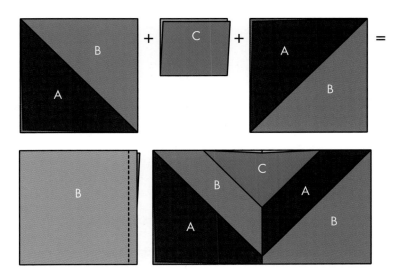

dimensional effect, leave the peeled-back portion over the E patches unsewn. Instead, sew across the fold on the first D piece, up over the E, then across the other D.

Fig. 2–76. A/B/C unit

Large Flower Blocks

Block center

1. For the dimensional pieces, fold 16 A squares and 32 F squares in half diagonally. Fold 16 C rectangles in half.

2. Use a glue-stick to secure a folded A square on 16 B squares.

3. Sew a folded C rectangle between two A/B units (fig. 2–76). Notice the rotation of the A/B units. Make eight.

4. Sew two folded C rectangles between two A/B/C units to complete the block center (fig. 2–77). Make four.

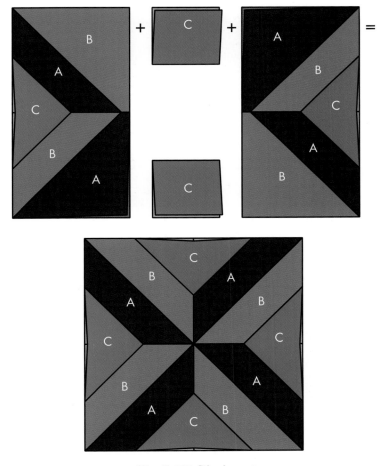

Fig. 2–77. Block center

Fig. 2–78. Frame unit, first step

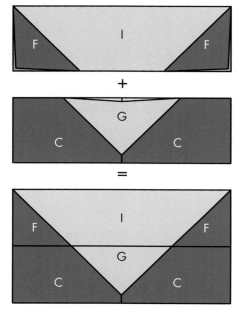

Fig. 2–79. Completed frame unit

Block frame

1. Fold 16 G rectangles in half. For the first step in making a frame unit, sew a folded G rectangle between two C rectangles (fig. 2–78). Make 16.

2. For the second step, use a glue-stick to secure two folded F triangles to an I rectangle. Make 16.

3. Sew this piece to the previous one to complete each frame unit (fig. 2–79).

Complete block

1. Sew a block center, four frame units, and four H squares together to complete a block (fig. 2–80). Make four.

2. Curve the C, F, and G pieces and double curve the A pieces (fig. 2–81, page 69).

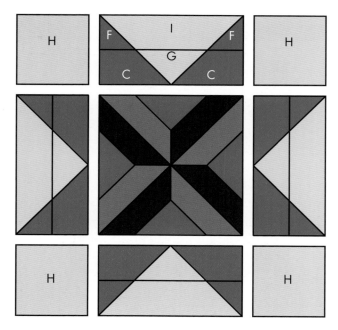

Fig. 2–80. Large Flower block

Make the Pieced Borders
Inner border

1. Fold 20 E rectangles in half. Sew a folded E rectangle between two J rectangles, as shown in figure 2–82, to make an E/J unit. Make eight.

2. Sew a folded E rectangle between two E/J units to make a border strip (fig. 2–83). Make four. Use two of these strips for the sides of the quilt.

3. At both ends of the other two border strips, sew an E rectangle between the strip and an H square (fig. 2–84). These strips will be used for the top and bottom of the quilt.

Fig. 2–81. Large Flower block with curves

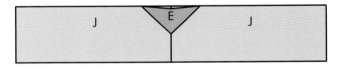

Fig. 2–82. E/J unit

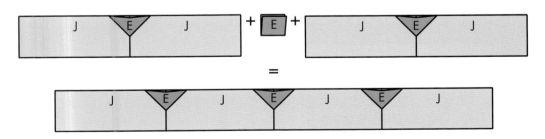

Fig. 2–83. Border strip

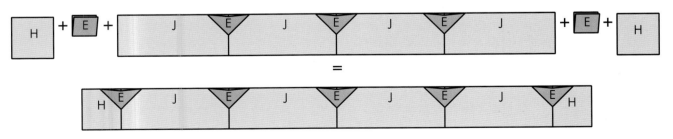

Fig. 2–84. Border strip with H squares

Fig. 2–85. Border unit 1, first step

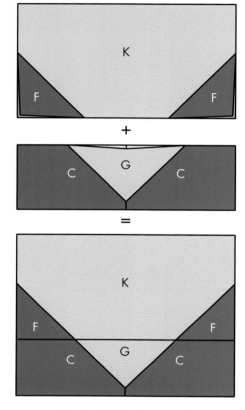

Fig. 2–86. Border unit 1

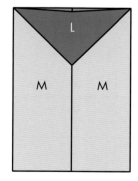

Fig. 2–87. Border unit 2

Outer border

1. Fold 20G and 16 L rectangles in half. Fold 40 F squares in half diagonally.

2. For the first step in making the unit, sew a folded G rectangle between two C rectangles (fig. 2–85). Make 20.

3. For the second step, use a glue-stick to secure two folded F triangles to a K rectangle. Make 20.

4. Sew the two pieces together to complete each border unit 1 (fig. 2–86). Make 20.

5. For border unit 2, sew a folded L square between two M rectangles, as shown in figure 2–87. Make 16.

6. Sew five of unit 1 and four of unit 2 together to make an outer border strip. Make four.

7. Sew an N square to both ends of two of the border strips. Curve the F and G pieces in each Unit 1 before the border is applied. (fig. 2–88, page 71).

Quilt Assembly

✦ Follow the quilt assembly diagram to join the blocks into horizontal rows. Then sew the rows together.

✦ Sew the inner border strips to the sides of the quilt. Sew the top and bottom inner border strips to the quilt, but leave the H square seams unsewn.

✦ Look at the inner border corners in the quilt assembly diagram. Using Y-shaped unit construction, add a folded E rectangle between the top border and each side border. Repeat for the bottom border.

✦ Sew an outer border strip to each side of the quilt. Sew the outer border strips with the N squares to the top and bottom. Curve the E and L triangles.

Finishing

✦ Sew the backing pieces together along their long edges.

✦ Layer the backing, batting, and quilt top. Quilt the layers. To enhance the flower designs, quilt around each one and heavily quilt the background. Leave the dimensional pieces unquilted to make them stand out.

✦ Join the binding strips and bind the raw edges.

Fig. 2–88. Quilt assembly

BEADED PRIMROSE

BEADED PRIMROSE, 65½" x 86½", made by the author

Peeled-Back Patchwork ~ Annette Ornelas

BEADED PRIMROSE

Skill level: ADVANCED

Finished block size: 12"

Finished quilt size: 65½" x 86½"

BEADED PRIMROSE is a great quilt for people of all ages. The blocks feature a special dimensional center that is folded before being pieced into the flower. This makes the rest of the curves a snap. BEADED PRIMROSE is also perfect for using up your scraps.

Before beginning, review Fabric Selection (page 8) and Dimensional and Curved Piecing (page10). Y-shaped unit construction is described on page 13.

Yardage and Cutting Requirements

Yardage (42" wide fabric)	First Cut (cut strips across the width)	Second Cut
Light green 2½ yds.	7 strips 2" 8 strips 3½" 7 strips 5½" (inner border)	80 rectangles 2" x 3½" (piece J) 31 rectangles 3½" x 9½" (piece K) ----
Medium green 2¾ yds.	7 strips 3½" 16 strips 2" 4 strips 2½" (outer border) 4 strips 5½" (outer border)	48 rectangles 2" x 3½" (piece C) 48 squares 3½" (piece D) 62 strips 2" x 9½" (piece G) ---- ----
Dark green 1¼ yd.	12 strips 2" 4 strips 3½"	240 squares 2" (piece F) 80 rectangles 2" x 3½" (piece H)
6 colors, ⅜ yd. each (make 2 primroses from each color*)	2 strips 3½" each color	24 rectangles 2" x 3½" (piece A) each color 8 squares 3½" (piece E) each color
Gold ¼ yd.	3 strips 2"	48 squares 2" (piece B)
Orange ⅓ yd.	4 strips 2"	80 squares 2" (piece I)
Binding ¾ yd.	8 strips 2"	
Backing 5⅜ yds.	2 pieces 37" x 91"	
Batting (90" wide) 2⅛ yds.	73" x 90"	

*To give your quilt a more scrappy look, make a few extra blocks in different colors. Then lay out and audition your blocks for the best color combinations and the most harmonious look.

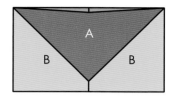

Fig. 2–89. Y-shaped A/B unit

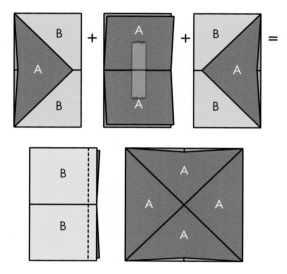

Fig. 2–90. Center unit

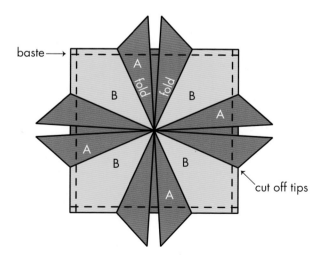

Fig. 2–91. Baste the edges and trim the points.

Making Primrose Blocks

1. For each primrose, fold four A and four C rectangles in half. Fold four D squares in half diagonally. (Dimensional pieces are always folded right side out.)

2. Using Y-shaped unit construction, sew one folded A piece between two B squares to make a Y-shaped A/B unit (fig. 2–89). Make two.

3. Place two folded A pieces between two Y-shaped A/B units, as shown in figure 2–90. (Pin or tape the folds so the pieces don't move during sewing.) Sew the pieces together and press the seam allowances open.

4. Grasp the folds of an A piece and fold them toward each other, as shown in figure 2–91. Repeat for the other three A pieces in the unit. The folds can be whatever distance apart you choose. Pin the folds.

5. Baste around the unit, approximately ⅛" from the edge. Remove the pins and cut off the folded tips (Fig. 2–91).

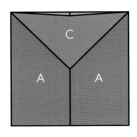

Fig. 2–92. Y-shaped A/C unit

6. Sew a folded C piece between two A rectangles to make a Y-shaped A/C unit (fig. 2–92). Make four.

7. Use a dab of glue to secure a folded D triangle on each of four E squares to make a D/E unit.

8. For each primrose block, join a primrose center, four A/C units, and four D/E units (fig. 2–93).

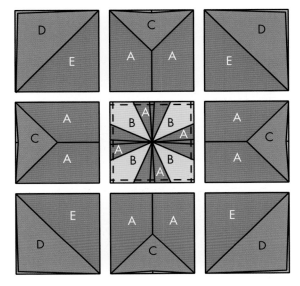

Fig. 2–93. Primrose block

9. Add a frame of four F squares and four G strips (fig. 2–94). Repeat steps 1–9 to make 12 blocks, a minimum of two from each flower color, or make more to choose from later.

10. Before the blocks are joined, curve piece C and double curve the folded D squares, as shown in figure 2–95, page 76. (For double curves, see page 16.)

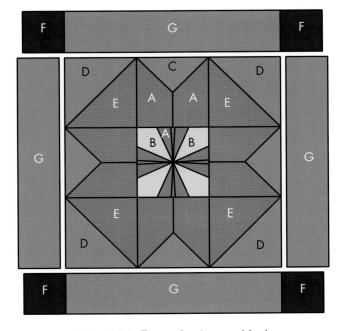

Fig. 2–94. Framed primrose block

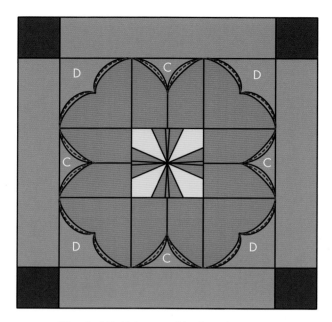

Fig. 2–95. Primrose block with curves

Fig. 2–96. Y-shaped H/I unit

Making Corner Flowers

1. Fold 80 H and 80 J rectangles in half.

2. Sew a folded H piece between two I squares to make a Y-shaped H/I unit (fig. 2–96). Make 40.

3. Place two folded H pieces between two Y-shaped H/I units, as shown in figure 2–97. (Pin or tape the folds so the pieces don't move during sewing.) Sew the pieces together and press the seam allowances open. Make 20.

4. Grasp one fold of an H piece and fold it again as shown in figure 2–98. Repeat for the other three H pieces in the unit. Pin the folds.

5. Baste around the unit, approximately ⅛" from the edge. Remove the pins and cut off the folded tips. Repeat steps 1–5 to make 20 corner flowers.

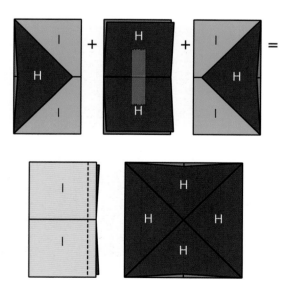

Fig. 2–97. Flower unit

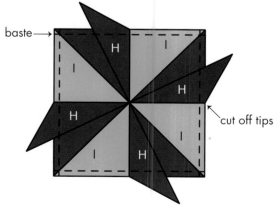

Fig. 2–98. Baste and trim the corner flower.

Making Lattice

1. Sew a folded J piece between two F squares to make a Y-shaped F/J unit (fig. 2–99). Make 80.

Fig. 2–99. Y-shaped F/J unit

2. Using corner flowers, Y-shaped F/J units, and F and G pieces, make the lattice units shown in figure 2–100a–d.

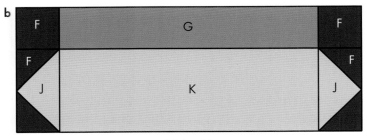

Make 31

Make 14

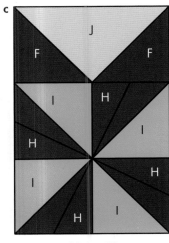

Make 10

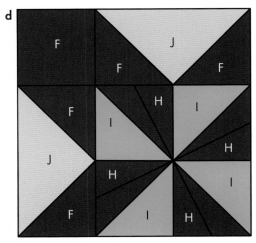

Make 4

Fig. 2–100. Lattice units: **(a)** unit 1, **(b)** unit 2, **(c)** unit 3, **(d)** unit 4.

Quilt Assembly

✦ Arrange the primrose blocks, corner flowers, and lattice units, as shown in the quilt assembly diagram (fig. 2–101, page 79). Sew the pieces together in horizontal rows. Join the rows.

✦ Cut one light green inner border strip in half. Sew a half strip to each of two whole strips.

✦ Measure across the center of the quilt and cut two whole strips this length. Sew these to the top and bottom of the quilt.

✦ Join the remaining light green inner border strips end to end to make two long strips.

✦ Measure down the center of the quilt and cut two inner border strips this length. Sew them to the sides of the quilt.

✦ To make the quilt longer and more suitable for a bed, the outer border is wider at the top and bottom than at the sides. Join two of the medium green 2½" outer border strips end to end. Repeat.

✦ Measure down the center of the quilt and cut both of the pieced strips this length. Sew the 2½" strips to the sides of the quilt.

✦ Likewise, join the 5½" outer border strips end to end to make two long strips. Measure, cut, and sew the 5½" strips to the top and bottom of the quilt.

Finishing

✦ Stitch the backing pieces together along the long edges.

✦ Layer the backing, batting, and quilt top. Quilt the layers. Leave the dimensional pieces unquilted to make them stand out. The more the background is compressed by dense quilting, the more the flowers will pop out. You can apply beads in the center of the primroses to enhance the flowers.

✦ Join the binding strips and bind the raw edges.

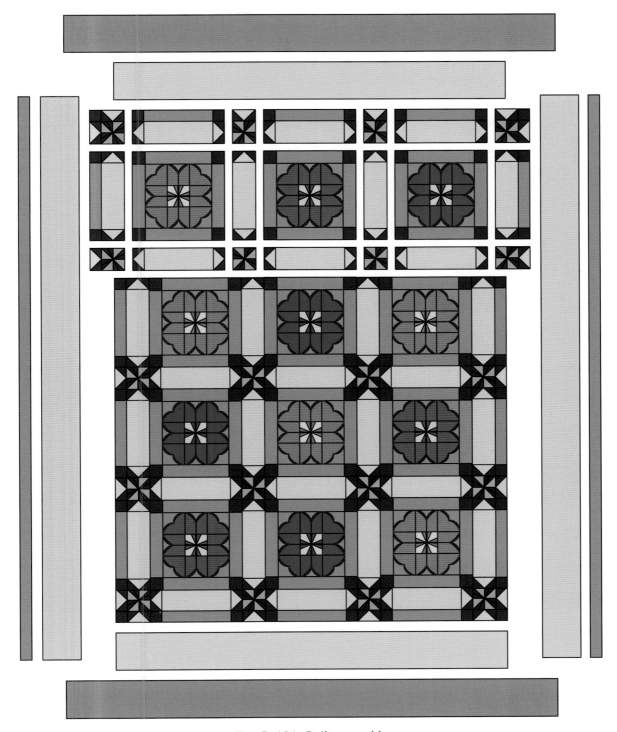

Fig. 2–101. Quilt assembly

FAIRY FLOWERS

FAIRY FLOWERS, 65½" x 65½", made by the author

FAIRY FLOWERS

Skill level: INTERMEDIATE
Finished block size: 12"
Finished quilt size: 65½" x 65½"

FAIRY FLOWERS features a different curved technique, which adds another dimension to the flower blocks. The quilt can be used as a wallhanging or a throw. When choosing fabrics, pay attention to the values. In this quilt, purple scraps were used to give the quilt dimension. Notice that all the purple scraps are of a similar value.

Before beginning, review Fabric Selection (page 8) and Dimensional Curved Piecing (page 10). Y-shaped unit construction is described on page 13.

Yardage and Cutting Requirements

Yardage (42" wide fabric)	First Cut (cut strips across the width)	Second Cut
Light tan 2⅞ yd.	4 strips 2" 9 strips 3½" 6 strips 3½" (inner border) 5 strips 6½"	72 squares 2" (piece H) 108 squares 3½" (piece F) ---- 8 rectangles 6½" x 12½" (piece I) 4 rectangles 6½" x 18½" (piece J)
Medium multi-print 1⅝ yds.	2 strips 2" 8 strips 5½" (outer border)	36 squares 2" (piece B) ----
Dark purple, 9 assorted fabrics, ⅛ yd. each	1 strip 3½" each fabric (flower petals)	From each strip, cut 4 rectangles 2" x 3½" (piece C) and 8 squares 3½" (piece G)
Dark purple ⅜ yd.	6 strips 1¼" (middle border)	----
Medium green ¾ yd.	6 strips 2" 2 strips 3½"	108 squares 2" (piece D) 36 rectangles 2" x 3½" (piece A)
Gold ⅜ yd.	2 strips 3½"	36 rectangles 2" x 3½" (piece E)
Binding ⅝ yd.	7 strips 2"	
Backing 4 yds.	2 pieces 36" x 70"	
Batting (90" wide) 2 yds.	70" x 70"	

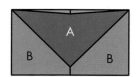

Fig. 2–102. Y-shaped A/B unit

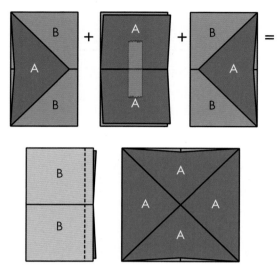

Fig. 2–103. A/B/A unit

Fig. 2–104. Y-shaped C/D unit

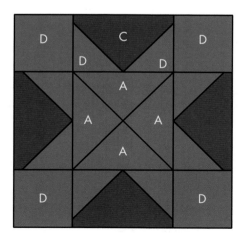

Fig. 2–105. Block center

Making Blocks

1. Fold the A, C, and E rectangles in half. Fold the H squares in half diagonally. (Dimensional pieces are always folded right side out.)

2. Sew a folded A rectangle between two B squares to make a Y-shaped A/B unit (fig. 2–102). Make 18.

3. Place two folded A pieces between two Y-shaped A/B units, as shown in figure 2–103. (Pin or tape the folds so the pieces don't move during sewing.) Sew the pieces together and press the seam allowances open. Make nine.

4. Sew one folded C rectangle between two D squares to make a Y-shaped C/D unit (fig. 2–104). Make 36.

5. Make three more units with C pieces of the same fabric. Repeat to make nine sets, one for each block.

6. Join an A/B/A unit, four C/D units, and four D patches to complete a block center (fig. 2–105). Make nine.

7. Sew one folded E piece between two F squares to make a Y-shaped E/F unit (fig. 2–106). Make 36.

8. Fold each Y-shaped E/F unit in half, right side out. Sew a folded Y-shaped E/F unit between two G squares as shown to make a Y-shaped E/F/G unit (fig. 2–107). Make 36.

9. Use a glue-stick to secure two folded H squares to each E/F/G unit to complete a flower petal unit (fig. 2–108). Make 36.

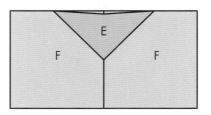

Fig. 2–106. Y-shaped E/F unit

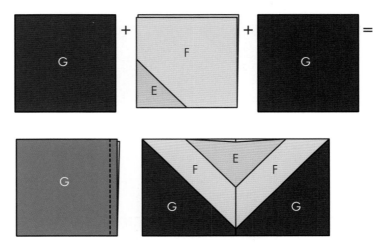

Fig. 2–107. Y-shaped E/F/G unit

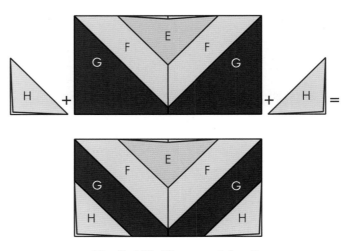

Fig. 2–108. Flower petal unit

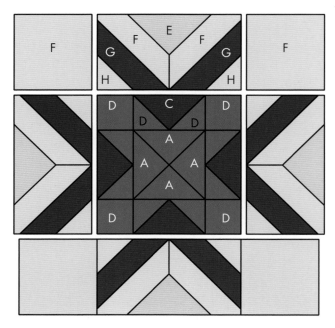

Fig. 2–109. Block assembly

Fig. 2–110. Block with curved pieces

9. Join a block center, four flower petal units, and four F patches to make a block. Make nine blocks (fig. 2–109).

10. Curve all of the folded inserts as shown in figure 2–110. For another dimensional effect, turn back the folded gold E pieces more than the others (see figure 2–91, page 74).

Quilt Assembly

◆ Referring to the quilt assembly diagram (fig. 2–111), sew the blocks and the I and J pieces together in horizontal rows. Then join the rows.

◆ Join the light tan inner border strips end to end as needed to make the borders. Measure down the center of the quilt and cut two border strips this length. Stitch these to the sides of the quilt. Measure, cut, and sew the top and bottom strips in the same way.

◆ Prepare, measure, cut, and sew the purple middle borders and the outer borders in the same way.

Finishing

◆ Stitch the backing pieces together along their long edges.

◆ Layer the backing, batting, and quilt top. Quilt the layers. To make the flowers stand out, quilt around but not over them.

◆ Join the binding strips end to end and bind the raw edges.

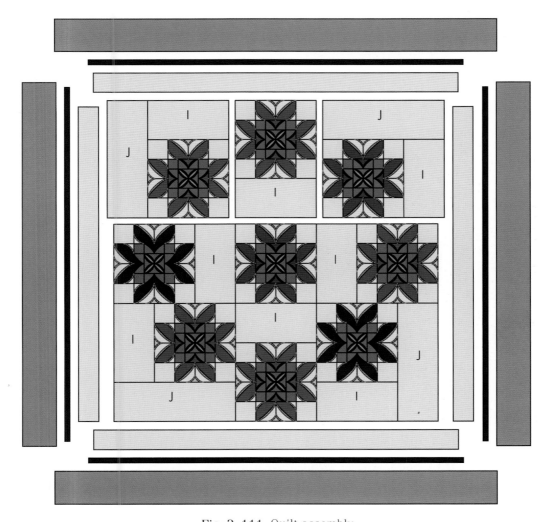

Fig. 2–111. Quilt assembly

FLY-AWAY

FLY-AWAY, 48" x 59", made by the author

Peeled-Back Patchwork ~ Annette Ornelas

FLY-AWAY

Skill level: ADVANCED
Finished block size with frame: 11"
Finished quilt size: 48" x 59"

FLY–AWAY is a whimsical and fun quilt. You have a choice of three different butterflies and a dragonfly. You can make as many of each one as you like. The wedge-shaped pieces that surround the butterflies and dragonflies make them twist in different directions.

Before beginning, review Fabric Selection (page 8) and Dimensional Curved Piecing (page 10). Y-shaped unit construction is described on page 13.

Yardage and Cutting Requirements

Yardage (42" wide fabric)	First Cut (cut strips across the width)	Second Cut
Black background (minimum combined total) 1½ yd.	(see individual butterflies and dragonfly)	
Wedge shapes* and border 1⅞ yds.	8 strips 3" 6 strips 6" (border)	24 strips 3" x 13½" (piece V)
Bright fabric 1 (sashing squares) ⅛ yd.	1 strip 1½"	20 squares 1½"
Bright fabric 2 (sashing squares) ⅛ yd.	2 strips 1½"	31 squares 1½"
Black (sashing) ½ yd.	9 strips 1½"	62 rectangles 1½" x 5½"
Binding ⅝ yd.	6 strips 2"	
Backing 3 yds.	2 pieces 32" x 53"	
Batting (90" wide) 1½ yds.	53" x 64"	

*Wedge shapes can be cut from scraps, if you prefer.

Butterfly 1 (each)

Yardage (42" wide fabric)	**Cut**
Black (background)	11 squares 1½" (piece A) 2 rectangles 1½" x 2½" (piece C) 2 squares 2½ (piece D) 2 rectangles 1½" x 3½" (piece I) 2 rectangles 1½" x 7½" (piece J) 2 rectangles 1½" x 9½" (piece K)
Bright scraps (wings)	2 squares 2¼" (piece E) 2 squares 2½" (piece G) 2 squares 3½" (piece H)
Medium scraps (head and body)	1 square 1½" (piece B) 1 square 2½" (piece F)

Butterfly 2 (each)

Black (background)	7 squares 1½" (piece A) 2 rectangles 1½" x 2½" (piece C) 2 squares 2½" (piece D) 2 rectangles 1½" x 7½" (piece J) 2 rectangles 1½" x 9½" (piece K) 4 rectangles 1½" x 2½" (piece L)
Bright scraps (wings)	2 squares 2¼" (piece E) 2 squares 2½" (piece G) 4 rectangles 2½" x 3½" (piece M)
Medium scraps (head and body)	1 square 1½" (piece B) 1 square 2½" (piece F)

Butterfly 3 (each)

Black (background)	5 squares 1½" (piece A) 2 rectangles 1½" x 2½" (piece C) 4 squares 2½" (piece D) 2 rectangles 1½" x 7½" (piece J) 2 rectangles 1½" x 9½" (piece K) 2 rectangles 1½" x 2½" (piece L)
Bright scraps (wings)	2 squares 2¼" (piece E) 2 squares 2½" (piece G) 2 rectangles 3½" x 4½" (piece N)
Medium scraps (head and body)	1 square 1½" (piece B) 1 square 2½" (piece F)

Dragonfly (each)

Yardage (42" wide fabric)	First Cut (cut strips across the width)
Black (background)	4 squares 2½" (piece D) 2 rectangles 1½" x 7½" (piece J) 2 rectangles 1½" x 9½" (piece K) 4 squares 2" (piece O) 2 squares 3½" (piece Q) 2 squares 3" (piece U)
Bright scraps (top wings)	2 squares 3½" (piece H)
Bright scraps (bottom wings)	2 squares 2½" (piece G) 2 squares 1½" (piece S) 4 rectangles 1½" x 3½" (piece T)
Medium scraps (head and body)	1 square 1½" (piece B) 1 square 2" (piece P) 1 square 3½" (piece R)

Making Butterflies

Choose how many butterflies and dragonflies you want to make. You will need a total of 12. Use the following directions to make all the butterfly head and body units, then add the wings, which are different for each butterfly. (All dimensional pieces are folded right side out.) Mark and stitch antennae to the butterflies, using bright thread, during the quilting process. Dragonfly instructions begin on page 95.

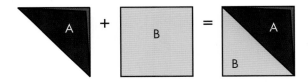

Fig. 2–112. A/B unit

Head unit (each butterfly)

1. Fold one A square in half diagonally. Use a glue-stick to secure the folded A square on a B square (fig. 2–112).

2. Add two C rectangles and a D square to the A/B unit to complete the head unit (fig. 2–113).

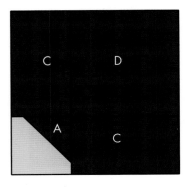

Fig. 2–113. Butterfly head unit

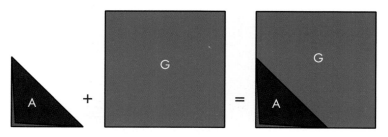

Fig. 2–114. A/G unit

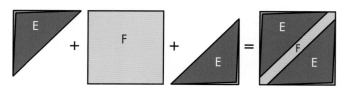

Fig. 2–115. E/F unit

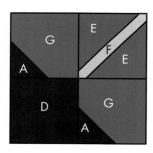

Fig. 2–116. Body unit

Body unit (each butterfly)

1. Fold two A and two E squares in half diagonally. Place a folded A square on a G square (small wing) and secure with glue. Make two A/G units (fig. 2–114).

2. Select an F square (body) to match the butterfly head. Use a glue-stick to secure two folded E pieces on the F square (fig. 2–115).

3. Join two A/G units, one E/F unit, and one D square to complete the body unit (fig. 2–116)

Wings (butterfly 1)

1. Fold eight A squares in half diagonally. Secure two folded A pieces to the body unit with a dab of glue (fig. 2–117).

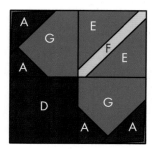

Fig. 2–117. Add folded A squares to the body unit.

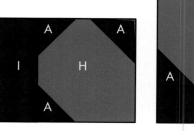

left wing   right wing

Fig. 2–118. A/H/I units

FLY-AWAY

2. Select two H squares (large wings) to match the small wings (pieces E and G) in the body unit.

3. Secure three A pieces to each H square. Sew one I rectangle to the side of each A/H unit (fig. 2–118, page 90).

4. Sew the head, body, and wing units together. Frame the butterfly with J and K rectangles to complete the block (fig. 2–119).

5. Curve the A pieces and double-curve the E pieces (fig. 2–120).

Wings (butterfly 2)

1. Fold four L rectangles in half. Fold four A squares in half diagonally.

2. Select four M squares (large wings) to match the small wings (pieces E and G) in the body unit.

3. Sew one folded L piece between two M rectangles to make a Y-shaped L/M unit (fig. 2–121).

4. Glue two folded A squares to complete a wing unit (fig. 2–122). Make two.

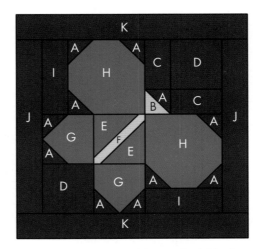

Fig. 2–119. Framed butterfly 1 block

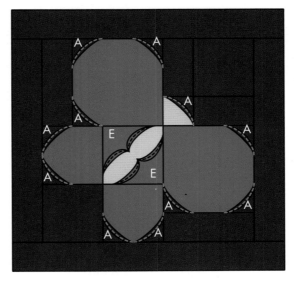

Fig. 2–120. Butterfly 1 block with curves

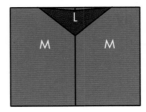

Fig. 2–121. Y-shaped L/M unit

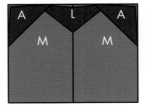

Fig. 2–122. Wing unit

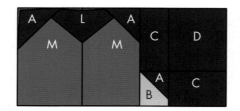

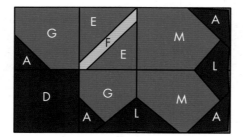

Fig. 2–123. Row 1

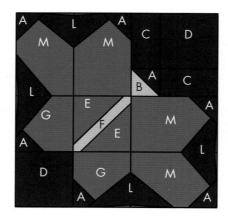

Fig. 2–124. Row 2

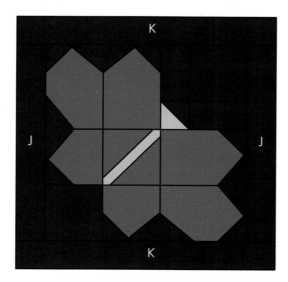

Fig. 2–125. Butterfly 2

5. Sew the left wing unit and the head unit together to make row 1 of the block (fig. 2–123).

6. Using Y-shaped unit construction, sew a folded L rectangle between the body unit and the right wing to make the second row (fig. 2–124).

7. To complete the butterfly, sew rows 1 and 2 together with a folded L inserted (Y-shaped construction) between the rows on the left side of the block (fig. 2–125).

8. Add rectangles J and K to frame the block (fig. 2–126).

9. Curve the A and L pieces, and double-curve the E pieces (fig. 2–127, page 93).

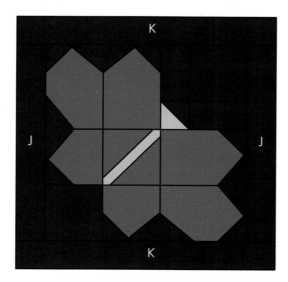

Fig. 2–126. Framed butterfly 2 block

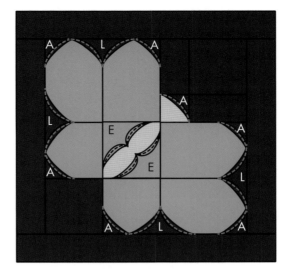

Fig. 2–127. Butterfly 2 block with curves

Wings, Butterfly 3

1. Fold two L rectangles in half. Fold two A and two D squares in half diagonally.

2. Select two N rectangles (large wings) to match the small wings (pieces E and G) in the body unit.

3. Glue a folded A triangle and a folded D triangle on each N square to complete the wing units. Make a left wing and a right wing unit (fig. 2–128).

4. Sew the head unit and the right wing unit together to make row 1 of the block (fig. 2–129).

5. Using Y-shaped unit construction, sew a folded L rectangle between the left wing unit and the body unit to make the second row (fig. 2–130).

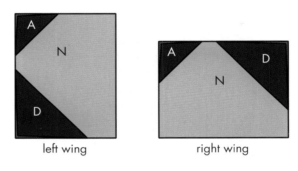

Fig. 2–128. Wing units

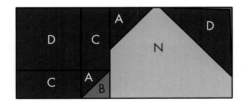

Fig. 2–129. Row 1

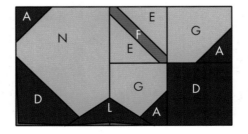

Fig. 2–130. Row 2

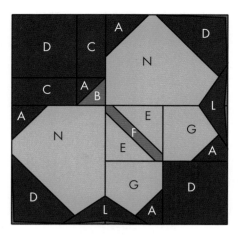

Fig. 2–131. Butterfly 3

6. To complete the butterfly, sew rows 1 and 2 together with a folded L inserted (Y-shaped unit) between the rows, on the right side of the block (fig. 2–131).

7. Add rectangles J and K to frame the block (fig. 2–132).

8. Curve the A, D, and L pieces and double-curve the E pieces (fig. 2–133).

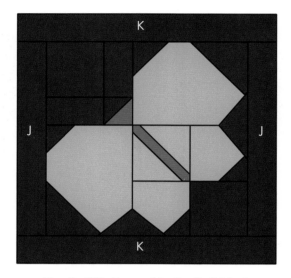

Fig. 2–132. Framed butterfly 3 block

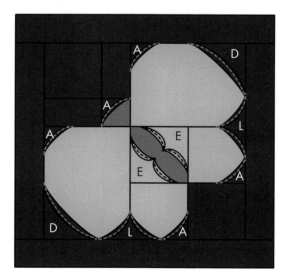

Fig. 2–133. Butterfly 2 with curves

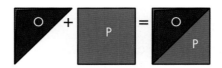

Fig. 2–134. O/P unit

Making the Dragonfly
Head unit

1. Fold all the D, G, Q, S, and U squares and one of the O squares in half diagonally.

2. Use a glue-stick to secure the folded O square on a P square to make an O/P unit (fig. 2–134).

3. Join three O squares and an O/P unit to complete the head unit (fig. 2–135).

Body unit

1. Secure two folded Q squares on an R square (body). Roughly dividing the unit in thirds, run two lines of basting stitches across the Q squares (fig. 2–136). These stitches will be used to hold the folds in place so they can be curved and stitched down in three sections.

2. Secure two folded S squares on a B square (body), as shown in figure 2–137.

3. Secure a folded D square on a T rectangle. Make a left and a right unit (fig. 2–138).

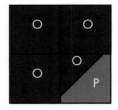

Fig. 2–135. Dragonfly head unit

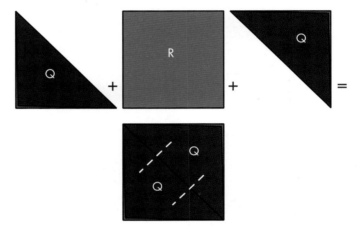

Fig. 2–136. Q/R unit with basting

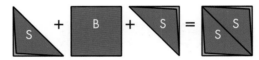

Fig. 2–137. B/S unit

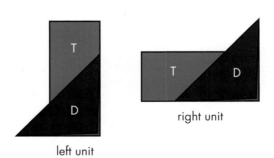

left unit

right unit

Fig. 2–138. D/T units

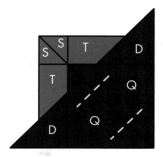

Fig. 2–139. Body unit

Fig. 2–140. G/H/U unit

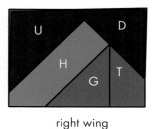

left wing

right wing

Fig. 2–141. Wing units

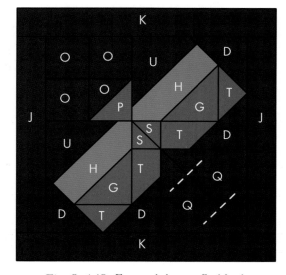

Fig. 2–142. Framed dragonfly block

4. Sew the Q/R, B/S, and D/T units together (fig. 2–139) to complete the body unit. Notice that the D triangles extend past the sides of this unit. They will be caught in the seams when the frame pieces are added.

Wing unit

1. Glue a folded U triangle and a folded G triangle to an H square to make a G/H/U unit (fig. 2–140). Make two.

2. Sew a T rectangle to each G/H/U unit and glue a folded D triangle to each unit to make a right and a left wing (fig. 2–141).

3. To complete the dragonfly, join the head, body, and wing units. Be sure to fold the D extensions out of the way so they are not caught in the seams when you sew the units together. Add the J and K frame units to complete the block (fig. 2–142).

4. Curve the D, G, O, S, and U pieces. Curve and stitch the dragonfly tail Q into three sections, using the basting stitches as a guide (fig. 2–143, page 97).

FLY-AWAY

Twisting the Blocks

1. Lay out your 12 butterfly and dragonfly blocks in a pleasing arrangement (fig. 2–144). Notice in the quilt assembly diagram that half of the blocks twist to the right and half to the left.

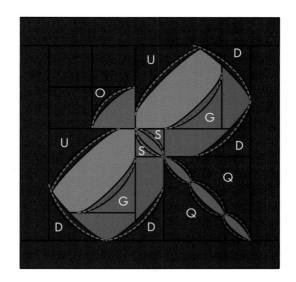

Fig. 2–143. Dragonfly with curves

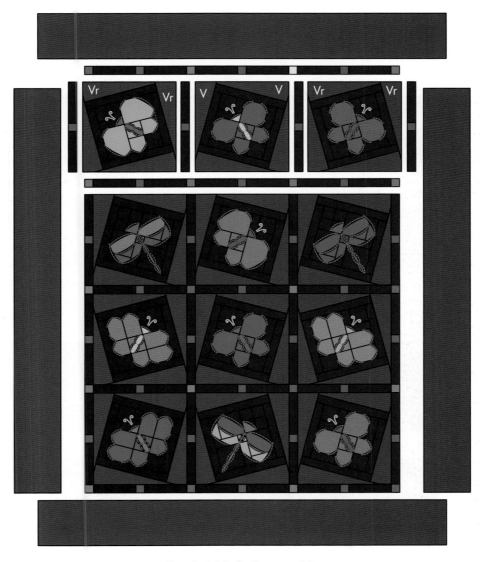

Fig. 2–144. Quilt assembly

2. Cut 12 of the V rectangles in half diagonally from upper-left corner to lower-right corner (V wedges). Cut the other 12 rectangles from upper-right to lower-left (Vr wedges), as shown in figure 2–145.

3. Sew the V and Vr wedges to the blocks to make six each of the left and right twists.

4. Trim each block to 11½", centering the butterfly or dragonfly in the block.

Quilt Assembly

✦ Referring back to the quilt assembly diagram (fig. 2–144, page 97), sew a sashing square between two sashing strips to make a sashing unit. Make 16 units.

✦ Join four sashing units and three blocks to make a block row. Make four block rows.

✦ Sew seven sashing squares and six sashing strips together, alternating types, to make a sashing row. Make five sashing rows.

✦ Join sashing rows and block rows, as shown, to complete the quilt center.

✦ Cut two border strips in half. Sew a half to the end of each border strip to make four long strips.

✦ Measure across the center of the quilt and cut two border strips this length. Sew these to the top and bottom of the quilt.

✦ Measure down the center of the quilt. Cut the two pieced strips this length and sew them to the sides of the quilt.

Finishing

✦ Sew the backing pieces together along their long edges.

✦ Layer the backing, batting, and quilt top. Quilt the layers. To make the butterflies and dragonflies stand out, quilt around, but not over, each one. A loop-de-loop design to simulate a butterfly's flight enhances the overall design. Add quilted antennae to butterflies, using contrasting thread.

✦ Join the binding strips and bind the raw edges.

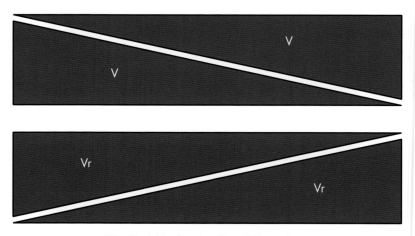

Fig. 2–145. Cutting V and Vr wedges

RIBBON AND ROSES

RIBBON AND ROSES, 86" x 86", made by the author

RIBBON AND ROSES

Skill level: ADVANCED
Finished block size: 21"
Finished quilt size: 81" square

Every year, my mother visits from Germany. The guest room is also my studio, which makes it hard to clean in advance. One year on the day of her arrival, the idea for this quilt popped into my mind. Instead of cleaning, I started designing. I felt like I was caught in the twilight zone – a magical moment where the puzzle pieces fall into place and nothing else can be done until the idea is brought to life. When my mom arrived that evening, I showed her the design. She agreed that RIBBONS AND ROSES was much better than a clean house.

Before beginning, review Fabric Selection (page 8) and Dimensional Curved Piecing (page 10). Y-shaped construction is described on page 13.

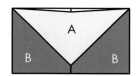

Fig. 2–146. Y-shaped A/B unit

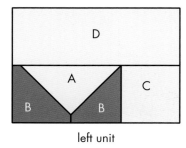

left unit

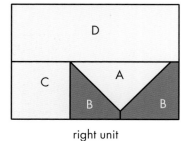

right unit

Fig. 2–147. Leaf unit

Making the Blocks

Fold 72 A and 72 H rectangles in half. Fold 36 G squares, all F squares, and 36 J squares in half diagonally. (Dimensional pieces are always folded right side out.)

Leaf unit

1. Sew a folded A piece between two B squares to make a Y-shaped A/B unit (fig. 2–146). Make 72.

2. Add a C square and a D rectangle to make a leaf unit (fig. 2–147). Make 36 left units and 36 right units.

ch Block: 8 cA, 8⊕H, rectangles
4 cG squares & 4 cF squares.

Christine Brady

Hickory Dickory Dock

Hickory Dickory Dock
The mouse ran up the clock
The clock struck one (**DONG**)
The mouse ran down
Hickory Dickory Dock

Light
= Light
= Light

ight
= 2" × 3½".
= 2' × 2".
= 2" × 5".
= 3½ × 3½.
=

Ribbon & Roses.

Bed = 55" × 80"
                21

²3 × 4

9/12 ?

Pink { 36.75 ÷ 9 = 4¼" per unit
      { 36⅝ × 42 = 1543.5 ÷ 9 = 171.5 = 4°?
      ⎩ 4·25×3 = 12·75 ÷ 42
      36·75 ÷ 9 × 12 = 49" = 2¼yds.

Red 36 × 42 = 1512 ÷ 9 = 168 ÷ 42 = 4" per un
                        1½yds.

Gold· 18 × 42 = 756 ÷ 9 = 84 ÷ 42 = 2" per unit
                        ¾yd.

Green = 36·25 × 42 = 1522·5 ÷ 9 = 169·2 ÷ 42 = 4·25"
× Aqua =   1¾ yd each.

Light = 216 × 42 = 9072 ÷ 9 = 1008 ÷ 42 = 24" per
                        8yds.

Yardage and Cutting Requirements

Yardage (42" wide fabric)	First Cut (cut strips across the width)	Second Cut
Pink 1⅝ yds.	8 strips 2" 9 strips 2" (strip piece) 4 strips 3½"	40 rectangles 2" x 3½" (piece I) 84 squares 2" (piece L) ---- 40 squares 3½" (piece G)
Red ⅞ yd.	12 strips 2"	112 rectangles 2" x 3½" (piece E) 40 squares 2" (piece K)
Gold ⅜ yd.	3 strips 2"	36 squares 2" (piece F) 4 rectangles 2"x 3½" (piece Q)
Green 1⅛ yds.	17 strips 2"	162 squares 2" (piece B) 108 rectangles 2"x 3½" (piece H)
Aqua 1⅛ yds.	7 strips 2" 9 strips 2" (strip piece)	40 rectangles 2" x 3½" (piece O) 66 squares 2" (piece P) ----
Light 6 yds.	33 strips 2" 15 strips 3½" 12 strips 3½" (strip piece) 7 strips 5"	160 rectangles 2" x 3½" (piece A) 196 squares 2" (piece C) 72 rectangles 2" x 5" (piece D) 92 squares 3½" (piece J) 36 rectangles 3½" x 6½" (piece N) 8 rectangles 3½" x 5" (piece R) ---- 36 rectangles 5" x 6½" (piece M) 4 squares 5" (piece S)
Binding ¾ yd.	9 strips 2"	
Backing 5 yds.*	2 pieces 43" x 85"	
Batting (90" wide) 2½ yds.	85" x 85"	

*If useable fabric width is less than 43", 7½ yds. will be needed.

Rose blossom

1. Place an E rectangle, wrong side up, in the position shown in figure 2–148. Fold the top left corner down. Make 36.

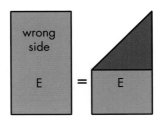

Fig. 2–148. Fold the top-left corner down.

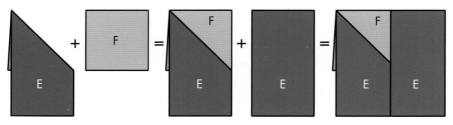

Fig. 2–149. E/F/E unit

2. Use a glue-stick to secure a folded E on an F square. Then stitch an E rectangle to the unit (fig. 2–149). Make 36.

3. Layer and sew a folded G square, a folded H rectangle (Y-shaped construction), and an E rectangle to the unit (fig. 2–150). Make 36. The G piece will cover the F piece completely until it is curved.

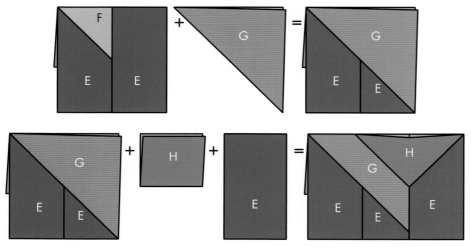

Fig. 2–150. E/F/G/H unit

4. Sew an I piece and a C piece together. Then use Y-shaped unit construction to sew a folded H rectangle between the I/C unit and the E/F/G/H unit to finish the flower center (fig. 2–151). Make 36.

5. Sew a flower center, two leaf units and a J patch together, as shown in figure 2–152, page 103. Then secure a folded J square to the bottom-left corner to complete the rose blossom. Make 36.

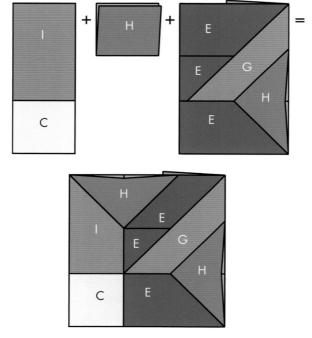

Fig. 2–151. Flower center

Block center

1. Fold 36 A rectangles in half. Fold 18 B, 36 C, and 18 P squares in half diagonally.

2. Secure a folded B square on an O rectangle with glue. Then sew a folded A rectangle between the B/O unit and an H rectangle (Y-shaped unit construction) to make a leaf section (fig. 2–153). Make 18.

3. Make a second leaf section in the same manner, but using the pieces shown in figure 2–154. Make 18.

4. Secure a folded C square to each leaf section (fig. 2–155).

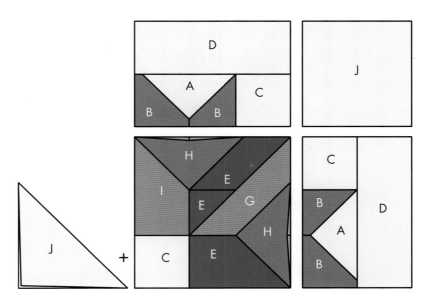

Fig. 2–152. Rose blossom assembly

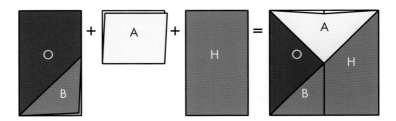

Fig. 2–153. Leaf section 1 assembly

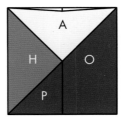

Fig. 2–154. Leaf section 2

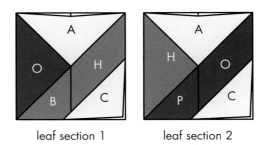

leaf section 1   leaf section 2

Fig. 2–155. Leaf sections with folded C squares

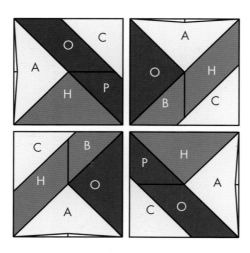

Fig. 2–156. Block center

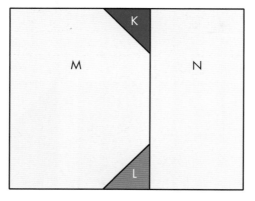

Fig. 2–157. Block side

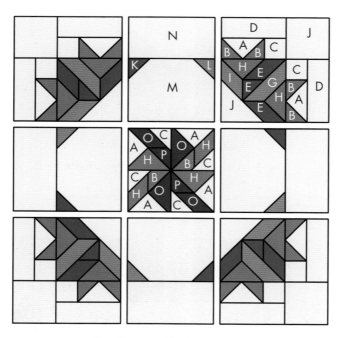

Fig. 2–158. Block assembly

5. Arrange units alternately in windmill fashion and stitch together like a four-patch (fig. 2–156). Make nine.

Block sides

Fold 36 K and 36 L squares in half diagonally. Secure a folded K square and a folded L square on an M rectangle with glue as shown. Then add an N rectangle to the unit (fig. 2–157). Make 36.

Block assembly

1. For each block, join four rose blossoms, four rose blossom sides and a block center (fig. 2–158).

2. Curve the folded A, B, C, E, and P pieces. Double-curve the G and J pieces (fig. 2–159).

Making Border Units

Border corner unit

1. Fold 16 A rectangles in half. Fold four G and four K squares in half diagonally.

2. Sew a folded K square between an E rectangle and a Q rectangle (fig. 2–160). Make four.

3. Place an I rectangle, wrong side up, as shown in figure 2–161. Fold the top-left corner down. Fold four.

4. Secure a folded I rectangle, right side up, on a C square (fig. 2–162). Make four C/I units.

5. Sew a 2" pink strip to a 2" aqua strip to make a strip-set. Press the seam allowances open. Make three strip-sets. Cut 48 sections, each 2" wide (two-patches) from the strip-sets (fig. 2–163).

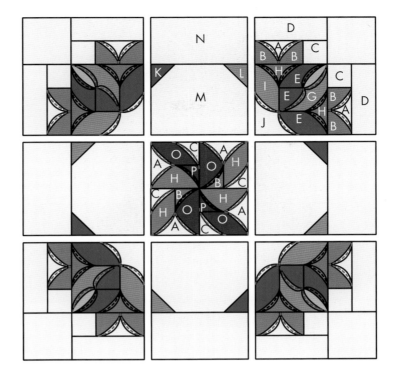

Fig. 2–159. Block with curves

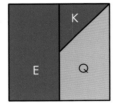

Fig. 2–160. E/K/Q unit

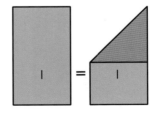

Fig. 2–161. Fold the top-left corner down.

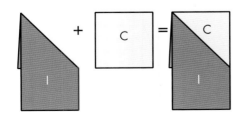

Fig. 2–162. C/I unit

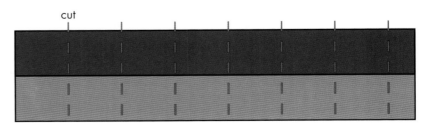

Fig. 2–163. Strip-set cut into 2" sections.

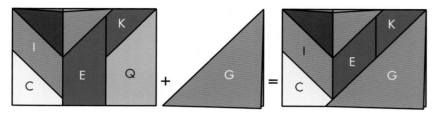

Fig. 2–164. Combined unit

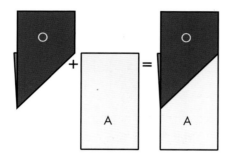

Fig. 2–165. Add a folded G square

Fig. 2–166. A/O unit

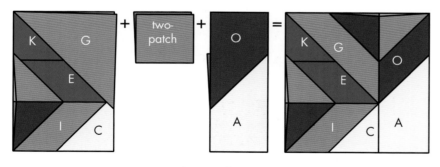

Fig. 2–167. Center unit

Fig. 2–168. Y-shaped P/A/L unit

6. Fold the two-patches in half, right side out. Use Y-shaped unit construction to sew a folded two-patch, pink side up, between a C/I unit and an E/K/Q unit (fig. 2–164). Make four combined units.

7. Secure a folded G piece on a combined unit with a dab of glue (fig. 2–165). Make four.

8. With an O rectangle wrong side up, fold the bottom-left corner up. Fold four. Secure a folded O on an A rectangle (fig. 2–166). Make four A/O units.

9. Using Y-shaped unit construction, sew a folded two-patch, pink side up, between a combined unit and an A/O unit to complete a center unit (fig. 2–167). Make four. Set aside the remaining two-patches.

10. Sew a folded A piece between a P square and an L square to make a Y-shaped P/A/L unit (fig. 2–168). Make 16.

11. Use a center unit, two P/A/L units, two C squares, two R squares, and an S square to complete each border corner unit (fig. 2–169, page 107). Make four. Set the remaining P/A/L units aside.

12. To complete the corner blocks, curve the folded A, I, K and O pieces and the two-patches. Double-curve the folded G pieces.

Border units 1 and 3

1. Use two light 3½" strips, a 2" pink strip, and a 2" aqua strip, in the order shown in figure 2–170, to make a strip-set. Make six strip-sets.

2. For unit 1, cut eight segments 9½" wide. For unit 3, cut 16 segments 8" wide.

Border unit 2

1. Fold 12 A rectangles in half. Sew a folded A piece between an L square and a P square to make the first section of border unit 2 (fig. 2–171). Make 12.

2. Sew a folded two-patch, aqua side up, between a P square and an L square to make the second section of the unit (fig. 2–172). Make 12.

3. Sew a folded two-patch, pink side up, between two C squares to make the third section (fig. 2–173). Make 12.

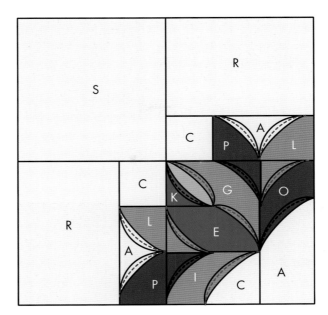

Fig. 2–169. Border corner unit

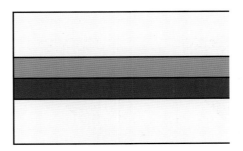

Fig. 2–170. Strip-set

Fig. 2–171. First section

Fig. 2–172. Second section

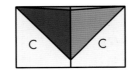

Fig. 2–173. Third section

4. Sew the sections together and add a J square and an A rectangle to complete border unit 2 (Fig. 2–174). Make 12.

5. Curve the folded A piece and the folded two-patches to complete the unit (fig. 2–175).

Border unit 4

Repeat the instructions for making border unit 2, but switch the color positions, as shown in figure 2–176. Make eight.

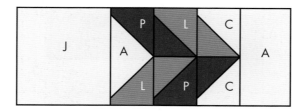

Fig. 2–174. Border unit 2

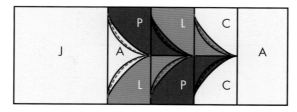

Fig. 2–175. Border unit 2 with curves

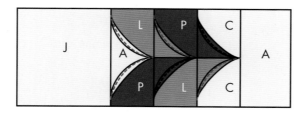

Fig. 2–176. Border unit 4 with curves

Quilt Assembly

Refer to the quilt assembly diagram (fig. 2–177, page 109).

Sew three blocks together to make a block row. Make three block rows, then sew the rows together.

✦ Join the blocks to make three rows of three blocks each. Join the rows.

✦ Join the border units to make a top, a bottom, and two side border strips. Stitch the side border strips to the sides of the quilt. Stitch the corner units to the top and bottom border strips. Then add these to complete the quilt top.

Finishing

✦ Stitch the backing pieces together along their long edges.

✦ Layer the backing, batting, and quilt top. Quilt the layers. Leave dimensional pieces unquilted to make them stand out.

✦ Join the binding strips and bind the raw edges.

corner unit

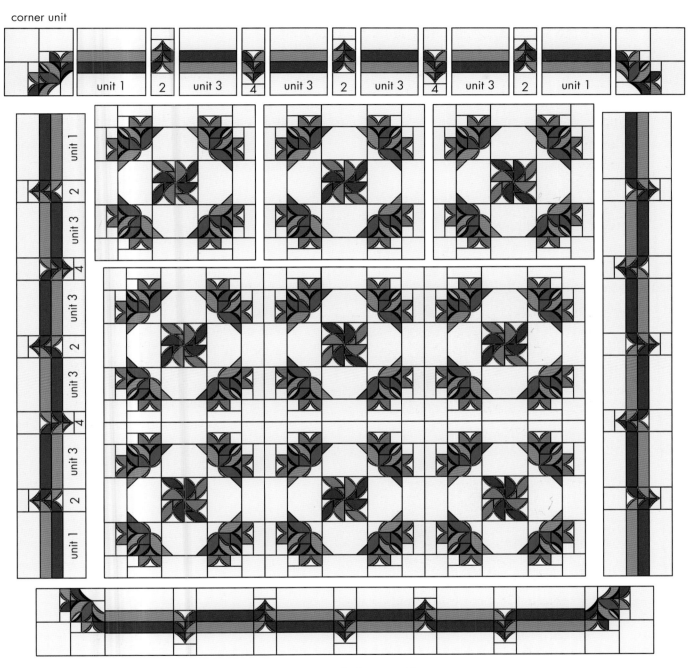

Fig. 2–177. Quilt assembly

Sources

Dimensional and curved patterns:

Annette Ornelas

Southwind Designs

5591 Lockridge Road

Fayetteville, NC 28311

910-630-2994

www.southwindquilts.com

annette@southwindquilts.com

Long-arm machine quilting:

Iris' Quilt Garden

8621 Birdseye Court

Linden, NC 28356

910-488-4228

arkomiris@earthlink.net

Fabric:

DYEnamic Fabrics

DYEnamic4u.@aol.com

(hand-dyes and batik fabrics)

Loving Stitches

www.lovingstitches.net

Design wall:

Quilter's Block Butler R

Can be purchased through

your local quilt shop or at

www.baysidequilting.com

About the Author

Annette Ornelas was born and raised in Germany. She has always expressed a special interest in art and textiles.

In 1991, when her husband was deployed to Desert Storm, Annette decided to enroll in a basic quilting course. Quilting quickly developed into a passion. When her husband, Mike, returned, he was very surprised to find their house was "quilted over." Stacks of fabric and quilts in various stages of completion had moved in and taken over the house. After being reassigned to Germany in 1992 and finding herself far removed from traditional quilting sources and her quilting friends, Annette explored her own quilting style.

In 1996 Annette started teaching in Fayetteville, North Carolina, where she earned a reputation for solving quilting problems creatively and putting her students at ease.

Annette has been published in *Quilter's Newsletter Magazine, Australian Patchwork and Stitching,* and *Australian Patchwork and Quilting*. She enjoys teaching all quilters of all skill levels and takes pleasure in finding ways to make quilting easy and fun for everyone. Annette finds inspiration in everyday things, especially flowers and nature.

Her dimensional and curved piecing techniques are a natural development from her experimentation with folded inserts. She aims to present complex-looking designs that are easy to piece, making curved designs achievable for all levels of quilters.

In 2000 Annette started her own pattern company, Southwind Designs, and has published over 25 patterns and a block-of-the-month series, Atlantis. Her line of patterns is being distributed worldwide. You may visit her Web site at www.southwindquilts.com.

Annette lives in North Carolina with her husband, Mike, and son, Kyle. She enjoys walking and gardening.

other AQS books

This is only a small selection of the books available from the American Quilter's Society. AQS books are known worldwide for timely topics, clear writing, beautiful color photos, and accurate illustrations and patterns. The following books are available from your local bookseller, quilt shop, or public library.

#6515   us$19.95

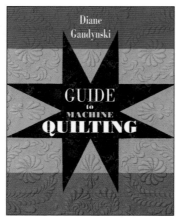

#6070   us$24.95

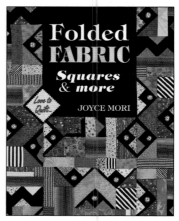

#6207   us$16.95

#6293   us$24.95

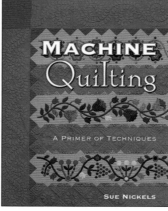

#6299   us$24.95

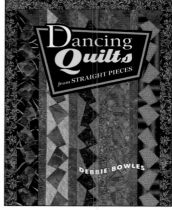

#6210   us$24.95

#6076   us$21.95

#5755   us$21.95

#6079   us$21.95

LOOK for these books nationally.
CALL or **VISIT** our Web site at

1-800-626-5420
www.americanquilter.com